Other works by Julian Sayarer:

LIFE CYCLES
MESSENGERS
INTERSTATE
ALL AT SEA
FIFTY MILES WIDE

IBERIA

BY JULIAN SAYARER

Fox, Finch & Tepper

Fox, **Finch** & Tepper

Published by Fox, Finch & Tepper Ltd
13-15 John Street, Bath, BA1 2JL
www.foxfinchtepper.com

First published by Fox, Finch & Tepper Ltd, 2021

1 3 5 7 9 10 8 6 4 2

Typeset in Bembo by Fox, Finch & Tepper Ltd
Printed and bound in Great Britain by TJ Books Ltd, Padstow, Cornwall

Cover Design by Tessimo Mahuta

ISBN 9780993046773

Iberia

Enceira

Coruche

Lisbon

Badajoz

Santa Amalia

Toledo

Cuenca

Valencia

Benicarlo

Barcelona

Spain + Portugal routes

Portugal   Atlantic
          Interior

Spain   Extremadura
       La Mancha
       Cataluna

For Sancho P

PORTUGAL

ATLANTIC

LUIS

I FIRST MET LUIS not long after riding into the north of Hungary, ten years ago as I pedalled towards Shanghai and he cycled – well, he wasn't sure where he was going. Luis was from Peru, a suburb outside Lima, and in the end he wound up riding to Moscow, where he worked some years without papers, washing dishes in kitchens, enjoying life, getting-by. At the time of our meeting, he had a line of dark black stitches, crossing his chin and that were just about holding, though being pulled at by the nasty wound he'd acquired when a gravelly descent in Albania slipped his wheels out from under him, and down he went. Luis had come-to from concussion, surrounded by villagers who loaded him into a truck and took him to a doctor, who stitched him up and would hear no talk of payment.

That day in Hungary, we rode together and shared old stories of riding in Albania. We talked of the total hospitality, agreeing that it was sometimes overbearing but probably, and literally, what the doctor ordered when in need of medical attention.

We camped a night in a recreation ground on the outskirts of a place called Győr, and next morning rolled into
town to sit through a serious café session of four coffees and
talk of the world, accompanied by bread and a budget Eastern European Nutella. Though still three months away, for
reasons I shan't trouble you with right now, I was on a tight
schedule to get to Shanghai, my first stop on my way around
the world, and as the third coffee was about to become the
fourth, Luis asked me:

"Are you sure you have time for another coffee?"

And I paused.

"What's the point in cycling around the world, if I don't
have time for another coffee with a friend?"

Luis would later go on to remind me that these were my
words, as I walked back in to get the coffee, and I would always be grateful to him for keeping the memory. It's nice to
be remembered well by others, memorialised in one of those
rare and glistening lines that we would like to think that we
live by, and we can at least take comfort in the fact that this is
how another is remembering us, even as we spend too many
of our days not quite living up to the line.

LISBON

THE SECOND TIME I MET LUIS was last week in Lisbon. I did not know he was here. He now has a scar on his chin and we talked, laughing, about the Albanian hospitality that is sometimes overbearing but, we agree, the sort of thing that is not only useful in a medical emergency, but also makes a life worth living.

Luis now has a girlfriend in Lisbon and a two-month old daughter. He has spent most of the last five years living in my beloved Istanbul, still getting-by, and still enjoying life. He tells me about his last ride; through Iran, Turkmenistan and into Central Asia. He reminds me of the things that I have forgotten and that it is sometimes the joy of forgetting to get to learn anew.

He reminds me that he dances tango, and tells me how he first met the mother of his child dancing tango in Lisbon. He tells me of the time, while he slept on sofas in Iran, of how he taught a secret tango class in Mashhad, one of the most religious cities in the country. I am grateful for all of my friends, but perhaps particularly those I met at the roadsides, and who were also pedalling. In them somehow is a secret photo of the world at its best.

Away from the table where we sit, outside and in open air, drinking our beers, there is a pandemic on. I shan't say much of it, for we have all heard enough of it already, and its scale is great enough that history will help remember it for us, without much need for me to elaborate on it here. Perhaps later I will write more of it.

I am supposed to go back to the UK, but although I left on an aeroplane, the claustrophobia of the idea seems too much for me right now. I do not like flying at the best of times, and right now is not the best of times.

"Why don't you ride?" Says Luis with a smile, and I look at him, slowly, like it's an extreme but also quite obvious idea.

"I don't know where I'd get a bike." I reply.

And Luis smiles again, like we both know that really isn't a problem.

BINA CLINICA

THERE ARE ALL KINDS OF CAMARADERIE that unite cyclists and lovers of bicycles around the world, but perhaps the most common element in the whole culture is the smell of rubber as you walk into a bike shop. It is the sort of smell that you stop noticing after a while of working in a bicycle shop, as I did as a teenager and for some of my twenties, but it is the sort of smell that then reminds you of being home whenever you return.

I remember a mechanic, one of the older ones, those enthusiastic collectors of all knowledge. Even then, he was a dying breed in the bicycle world – replaced by younger men and women, with better tattoos, better dentistry and less knowledge – and he explained to me that the rubber smell is accentuated by the smell of dried, powdered fish scales, which are put inside inner tubes to serve as a sort of talc that absorbs any humidity. Rubber and fish scales, then. It is no boutique, but you'd miss this smell if it were gone.

Bina Clinica is to cities what this smell is to bicycle shops. You will always find it. It is next to the railway tracks, perhaps the wrong side of them. It is in an old warehouse space, set in one of a row of factory units from the days when cities made things other than flat whites and vegan wraps. It is piled high with used bicycles waiting for repairs and then to be loved again. It is piled as high with loved bicycles waiting for a mechanic's touch.

At the back of the space is a workshop behind wooden countertops that – out of sight – I would put money on being constructed on top of salvaged pallets. There are large, cast iron blue vices, wheels in wheelstands, and everything is somehow covered with the shining grey veneer of oil.

This bicycle shop is a universal one. As universal as its smell of rubber, it exists from New York City to Melbourne to Santiago. It is a place where the misfits of a community, people who don't quite fit a world of cars or a world of consumerism, come to gather. One day they will be driven-out by the landowner needing to charge some sort of a commercial rent, and then they will be replaced by a café. If – that rare thing – the landlord is decent, this day will come later and reluctantly, but it will come. If the owners of the shop are lucky or smart enough, they will just in time invest in a coffee machine, and put some tables outside, so that they can ride this transition and be both bike shop and café. For a while.

Eventually, as inevitable as the force of gravity that once pulled Luis from his bike on an Albanian mountainside, the units will be demolished to make way for luxury flats that will have no soul and none of us will ever own or visit. This is just destiny, but it is our job to resist that destiny for as long as possible. And meanwhile, it is our sworn duty to give our custom to Bina Clinica for as long it shall exist. By the time it is gone, another will exist elsewhere, in a part of town we once wouldn't have thought to visit. I promise.

After some back-and-forth, a woman who runs the shop, whose name I do not catch and regret not doing, leads me outside to a blue bike with the pannier rack that is in truth all I need.

"We have this one."

I look at it. A mountain bike, but, as I lift it, not too heavy. The tyres are knobbly, more traction than I need – will slow me down.

"Can you change the tyres?"

In Portuguese, she calls back to a mechanic in the workshop. He puts down what he is working on and walks out, lifting two tyres from a hook on the wall. They are fastened with a piece of paper that says €10. They are Schwalbe, Marathon Plus, and he smiles at me as he says it, but I think he rightly guesses that I know what this means.

"Second-hand, but they are good."

I talk a little longer with the woman outside, who leads me inside to look at accessories on a further wall. I pull down a bottle cage and a bottle, which – for all the big money and the bespoke recommendations – are truly the only essential accessories you need to ride a long way. Then, the next most essential things; I take a puncture repair kit and then tyre leavers, chunky and yellow – Pedros. A brand, but, I concede, the best brand.

"Are these your only levers?"

"Yes," she pauses. And I smile as she smiles, again knowing that I know, as if these names and items form a language all of their own.

She says it, straight: "But they are the best."

At the counter she rings it up. €125.40 for the bike and accessories. She sweeps the tyre levers and puncture kit towards me.

"But these I give to you as a gift." She pulls a business card from its plastic holder on the countertop. "But if you tell us when you get home, it is nice."

I take the card, I take my gift. "Thank you. And can we call it €130?" and I gesture to her and the mechanics, "so you can have some beers from me after work, to say thank you."

She nods with a surprised smile, thanks me. And between our reciprocal gifts, our little bicycle bartering and kindnesses in-kind, a little of the circle of life continues.

CAMPO

IT IS ONLY WHEN I AM CYCLING that I truly come to life, when I see the world as it could be, and I breathe again. Portugal opens for me, and I relish the knowledge that I have no precise timetable nor even destination. For now, I can just ride. In terms of direction, my only real thought is that north up the coast I go up and down the glorious but high orange cliffs, while turning east I could instead ride the flats of those river valleys that make their ways finally out between the cliffs and to the ocean.

Beyond this, I do not know. I may head towards friends who just left London for Barcelona. Perhaps I will spend a night on the balcony I like to imagine their new flat will have, and we can grill courgettes and chorizo on the coals of a barbecue we'll light there. I may head further northeast, into France and then Dieppe; that road to the port I know so well, past the cidery of Monsieur Gentilhommière, who prints his name on the green glass bottles of his apple elixir, which it is impossible to drink without a smile also moving over your lips. Alternatively, I may make a more direct route to Galicia,

Santander, and then the boat to Devon, riding home through the apples and cideries of my own country.

On a bicycle, the map seems suddenly dressed in opportunity; I see the world anew. Detail presents itself, and as ever the world comes alive in the places between the places; between the ports and the metropoles, where life still happens in ways that defy the clichés of contrived events and image-conscious images, by which media, marketing and surveillance now remake our cityscapes. An old man sits at a bus stop and plays the flute. And my soul drinks from this sight.

My bicycle has a name already. It is the first of my bicycles that I have named for some time, because in order to name a bicycle it must have character and to acquire character a bicycle needs a story. It is hard to name an expensive bicycle, because an expensive bicycle has less character. The expense normally buys a bicycle that, in its very reliability, removes the idiosyncrasy and the minor but lovable flaws in which stories are born. It's not the bicycle's fault, that's just the way it goes.

My bicycle is blue, pure blue, the colour of the Atlantic now beside me with the sun on it. It is a blue that makes me think instinctively of 'Kind of Blue', the Miles Davis album, which is beautiful but also speaks to some of the sadness that the world right now has in it. And so the bicycle, I decide, is to be called Miles, because I also hope that it will carry me well enough across enough of them.

Miles is not, I soon realise, in particularly great health, though he is passable. The gears rattle more than I first noticed, though this is maybe down to a bent axle at the crank, or perhaps a chain-ring that once took a heavy blow. I worry that lurking here might be too many stories.

I look down at the axle and chain-ring, trundling, moving in and then out with each pedalled orbit. What this bicycle needs is one of those French mechanics; those gentle ogres with a moustache, dressed in grimy overalls and smoking a cigarette with a long column of ash hanging from it, where he stands in the doorway of his shop which smells of rubber, but also of cigarettes. He will take my bicycle and its slightly bent chain-ring, and he will remove the offending part and put it on his worktop in his large, cast iron blue vice. He will lift a hammer, and then with what seems like great brutality but is actually the learned precision of a surgeon, he will deal a new and almighty blow to the offending area, after which it will no longer be bent, and will run smoothly forever.

This mechanic exists, but I have not found him yet.

As I ride, I realise that the levers for the gears are set too centrally on the handlebars, so that they press a little at where my hands grip. This, at some point, I can adjust myself, but for now, I make a truce with it, for this is my machine; this is what I must work with. There are advantages to having a fine bicycle in perfect working order - with such a machine you can try to go faster. With a fine bicycle you can test the limits of your physical performance, while with a passable bicycle you test the limits of your patience.

Miles, in good enough working order but hardly fine-tuned, will test my mind, my ability to find a contentment in that which is mine above that which I desire. Miles will train my mind not to wander to the small things that bother it but probably shouldn't. It is in this kind of a machine that you learn to make peace with your bicycle, with that which you have, and ride over the land.

LOVE — ERICEIRA

AT THE BEACH are a man and a woman, pensioners, an old couple.

She has short curls of hair, silver all over, and she lies on her back on a towel. Her body is bronze and plump and wrapped in the skin of a black bathing suit. She is beyond the age of a conventional beauty, but exudes the grace of an indifference to it. Why do we understand beauty as an aesthetic quality? Is ease not beauty? Is peace not beauty?

Resplendent she reclines, on her back, like a queen or a maharani of this little cove. Her husband he lies also on his back, though using his wife's soft belly as a pillow. A baseball cap rests on his forehead and shields his eyes, and from his open shirt shoot lengths of chest hair that climb to the height of his chin and seem like they will never stop growing. I look at them both a moment more, and he reaches behind him into the hardened plastic box of a picnic cooler. He hands her food, and as naturally as if she were breathing, she takes it without looking round.

Between them, I think, is some picture of perfect marital bliss.

This must be what love looks like.

HUMILITY

FROM THE CLIFF I LOOK OUT, out at the Atlantic; at the ends of Europe, at the ends of the Earth. I strain my eyes, looking out at the ocean, and I can just glimpse a beach of white sand, Edisto, where once I slept, as a younger man but still beside a bicycle, on the opposite shore in South Carolina.

I think of how Portuguese must always have done this, this looking-out; a ready willingness to sail off into the unknown and expect to find something, ever since the time of Vasco da Gama. I consider that fact; that the oldest ally of Britain is Portugal. This was because of their shared utility in the common enemy of Spain across the centuries, but also due to the advanced navies of both, and the logic of not making enemies of those who could also wield power at sea. I consider that name, Portuguese Man of War, and that such a deadly jellyfish was given it must say something of the ferocity of the Portuguese navy and its sailors of old. I imagine them, with cutlasses and sabres, taking to ropes and swinging aboard my ship.

Once, in Istanbul, the other side of Europe, a more careful student of history than I explained to me that the Ottoman Empire stagnated – in political, organisational and technological terms – in part because of the riches of the Mediterranean. Its calmer seas, its fertile soils, the spices that stretched from Sana'a, Yemen; to Gaziantep; to Marrakech. Its coffee, its soap from Aleppo, the glories of Istanbul, Beirut, Damascus, the port of Palestine at Jaffa, the riches of Africa and Asia beyond. The Ottomans had less need to innovate new means of extraction, because everything was right there, and so – I suppose – they innovated not for discovery, but for comfort and opulence instead.

I wonder, what is Portugal? Is it Mediterranean, a sea it hardly touches and yet a people with which it seems so similar? Or is it Atlantic, most of the states of which are so very different to this one and its relaxed appreciation for life?

You will have to forgive me my history. Guilty as charged; I am a generalist. The world to me is a scattered place that sometimes by dint of a chance encounter or piece of knowledge sometimes makes sense; panning brackish water for rare gems of truth. But perhaps this is only the true nature of the world anyway.

Above all else, my advice in understanding the world, in so much as anyone can, is to take friends from all around it, and ask them questions until the point at which they almost tire of you.

Sometimes I think I am at an advantage because my friends have often been cyclists; riders of the bicycle, an order all of its own. In a cyclist is where best of all you will find an explanation of something so complex as a country. In my experience, it is cyclists, especially touring ones, who best possess that perfect balance of indifference to formal politics but attention to it; that equal respect for the outside world in its wonder and inner mind in its cerebral ways. A cyclist relies on a bicycle but only to ride it, and in this is created the basic tendency to hold respect for systems and engineering, but only in so much as the purpose they serve, and how effectively they serve it. As for bicycles, so should it go for rights, for democracy, for all systems of order and thought.

Sometimes all my collaging of information bothers me. My head flits with the passing roadside. I envy and respect the specialists; their expertise first and salaries second. Other times, I consider those many supposed experts unable even to join one dot to an adjacent dot, or see beyond the line of their nose and the book, or the single point of note, beneath it. Our politics has been ordered for specialisation, and even a very shallow form of it, where things, ideas and people are each looked at in isolation, which then makes them easier to prise apart. Atomised.

What, then, is Portugal in this gaze of mine? This broad roadside anthropology that I have practiced so far and wide now, under the microscope of the off-hand remark or gesture, the textbook of only the road and the café?

Firstly, and forgive me such a bromide – but the country seems both quiet and loud. I feel that when people speak they are quieter than normally so in Europe, or anywhere else I know, but when they grow loud then so are they louder. The language itself seems to operate in softness, in tones that hush naturally. Despite that, arguments, and even basic excitements that are not arguments, seem quickly to grow very loud. People shout in the streets when they need to, in a way that is at odds with the northern European bourgeoisie, who can imagine nothing worse than drawing attention to themselves, apart from not being given attention as a right. This loudness, combined with the friend who told me jokingly that most rural Portuguese properties have an illegal extension, built without permission, at the rear of the house, reminds me – along with the thick black hair, dark eyes, skin and brow of so many faces, and the ceramic tiles of beautiful patterns adorning so many walls – that Portugal was once of the so-called Middle East, the Arab World.

On the road behind me; the Algarve, a word I have heard most often in the British accent of silver-haired pensioners recounting a holiday. But the origin of Algarve is Al Gharb, Arabic for "The West", when all Iberia was within the Umayyad Caliphate, and made up its westernmost point. The expulsion of the Jews from Iberia remains well-remembered in Western history; the shadow of the Inquisition is strong. Portugal and Spain now restore passports and citizenship to the descendants of their persecution, while the Muslim sisters and brothers the Jews were expelled alongside go mostly forgotten. What makes a memory, and what makes us forget? I am told that in Portugal, people prefer no more to talk of these histories, as if by now they are all just awkward family secrets.

Other people go beyond my generalisations and brief accounts in describing this country and its past. I was once told that the Portuguese are not 'self-confident', have 'low self-esteem'. And even for me, such a casual, fleeting scholar as I am, I wonder how anyone could ever express the psyche of ten million individuals in such broad terms? Saudade, that word of Portuguese so borrowed and well-travelled – does it describe more than only the nostalgia for a better place and time felt deep inside so many of us? Did the tallest kid in Portuguese class, unlike all those like him around the world, really not have some sort of swaggering self-confidence, superficial and unearned as it might have been? Or was it simply less swaggering? I am told, typically enough, that as a poor country, the Portuguese now love to buy and drive cars; a social marker as it is for still-poor people everywhere; a display that they have escaped their former poverty but now give their disposable income to car, oil and insurance companies instead. A Portuguese man in a bar will tell me, as we discuss the bar's ostentatious decoration, "yes, we are pretentious. People get money and right away they want you to know it."

I think of Ronaldo, that footballer from the South Lisbon tenement blocks, one of those neighbourhoods with the external stairwell fire exits, where the seagulls sit atop of chimney pots like chess pieces, and you go down through the washing lines, down through the balcony railings and then the man in a vest always smoking on his doorstep, down through to where the child's ball bounces on the street beside the wrong side of the tracks.

He was once the best and richest footballer in the world, but came to be so disliked for his displays of wealth, having grown up poor. Often, he was shielded by his manager, himself the son of Govan shipbuilders in Glasgow, and thus the pair united in the universality of what it is to be working class. The manager articulated how much of the criticism was about no more than social class, including from other Portuguese.

For those born poor, the acquisition of wealth is often seen as a crime in itself; a dishonourable cheating of the fate that decrees you should also be willing to die that way.

I think of more logical roots to this apparently low self-esteem. Exhibit A; one word, a name: Salazar; dictator here until 1974. I think there must be few better ways to crush self-esteem than dictatorship and its thuggery, which ordains how you, an individual, a human, have no right to be heard, nor to govern your own affairs, nor to look out on all the other men and women as equals. Perhaps this might genuinely destroy the self-esteem of an entire nation.

Then the counter-argument, Exhibit B; the fact that the Portuguese were not only ruled over; they also ruled, great swathes of the world. How does a country enact dominion over tracts of the world and not grow swaggering, conceited by empire? When I asked this once, I was told that this was because the Portuguese created empire through 'puta e vinho', whores and wine. Portugal's imperialism was not – so the theory, perhaps generously, goes – primarily a warring one, but only the creation of the world's first soft power. That empire, too, was staffed by the army. Unlike the French in Algeria, Jewish settlers to Palestine, and British in India, Portugal did not en masse send a civilian population to live as a colonial elite, as higher-ups to the native, local population. In not doing so, Portugal did not train itself so deeply in supremacy, and so, when empire ended, it did not import that supremacy and its logic back to Portugal.

When empire ended? And there waits my greatest fascination with Portugal – how a nation could rule over the world and still wind-up humble. The Portuguese empire ended with neither a bang nor a whimper, but that most rare and quietly dignified of things – an apology. Portugal did not simply 'give back' its colonies – in so much as anyone can ever 'give back' something that was never rightfully theirs to begin with – but it left those colonies, and it left them with that one word, often the hardest to say. "Sorry."

Portugal did not, as the French, fool itself into believing it brought with it some civilisation. It did not, as the British, lie to itself that it brought engineering and opportunities – the famous railways. It did not, as the Israelis in Palestine or Boers in apartheid South Africa, claim that the land it took had been empty. And it did not, as the United States of America, believe that the bombs it dropped and drops still, bring freedom from tyranny to those they fall upon. Portugal said "sorry", and then left, taking with it a recognition of wrongdoing, and the nearest a state can get to decency when exiting the evils of empire.

There is only one other state that, in my mind, has taken a path that reminds me of this one: Germany. The extremities of the Second World War, the industrial murder and destruction, not to mention defeat – for there is nothing like the conditions of those we must submit to for creating contrition – all obliged Germany to accept both culpability for the War, and in it the notion of nationalism as a force that, pursued, culminates in great evil, and so must be feared and often resisted for its potential to lead there. Lisbon said "sorry", Berlin built memorials to its own horrors, to the Murdered Jews of Europe, and – even if that monument excludes so many others killed by the million in Nazi death camps – both cut a line, severed a cord, connecting future to past. In so doing, they free the future to pursue better things, liberated from the suffocation of nostalgia, or the contortions of truth inflicted by a nation's need to romanticise itself, to see itself as intrinsically good.

So what is this 'self-esteem' the Portuguese supposedly lack? Is confidence the ability or need to puff ourselves up beyond our natural size, to take more space? And why would such a thing be seen as a strength and not a weakness; the fear to simply come as we are? What is confidence, if not to meet the world with discretion, and presume from it decency in return?

Riding with these thoughts, I consider Dannish.

Dannish was a young boy, seventeen years old, his parents immigrants to East London from Bengal. He was another of the world's poor who told me once, as we worked on his bicycle at a London workshop, of how he loved cycling, but would drive a car when he grew up.

That day in the workshop had been the one before a youth club's bike ride, from the city of London and to the coast at Brighton. Without much money in the family to buy his own, Dannish had used a borrowed bicycle perhaps four years too small for him, in order to take part in the ride. His stout legs rose most of the way up and beyond the handle bars as we pedalled together through Sussex.

On his hands, Dannish wore a pair of decorator's gloves; woven thick from cotton and with plastic dots across the palms and fingers, intended to help grip a paint brush or a spatula pressing putty into cracks. Dannish had to wrestle the whole bicycle from side to side up each hill.

"I just gotta make it," he said, again and again. "I just gotta make it."

To Dannish, all life was a challenge, one that he met with a smile but in which he was always determined to succeed. The hills were like the universities he dreamt of getting entry to, and I rode beside him, listening to the oaths he muttered to himself as the hills kept coming.

"I gotta be confident, I gotta be confident."

And I listened, thinking the boy seemed almost burdened by this expectation of himself.

I turned to him and smiled, bicycles rolling under us; "Dannish, you don't have to be confident."

"Why not? What else should I be?"

"Just be humble, Dannish. Be humble, and keep going."

"Humble," he said, still fighting pedals. "That's a good word."

CAMINO

A MAN WALKS TOWARDS WHERE I SIT, eating an orange. He has a backpack on, Nordic walking poles in either hand, proper shoes; professional walking attire, like he walks all hours of the day for an occupation, or at least, for a while he will. His black skin has tan lines from the hot sun and what looks like long days under it. Around one wrist is a wrap of fabric he lifts to mop his brow. He heads north, gives a small smile, and the aura around him is unmistakable: the Way of Saint Jean, Santiago de Compostela. Pilgrim. That route where we dump out so much of our misery and stress and fear, across the centuries, and still it retains its beauty, as if nature can dissolve all our human ailments.

I once had a friend in Birmingham; a teacher in a failing school and with a nervous breakdown always like a slow train coming. Recreational drug use was, as always, the standard, quiet self-medication prescribed informally throughout the UK and its working culture. One Thursday he was buckling worse than normal. Friday the last day of term. Friday night a bag of cocaine, snorted to himself. Saturday morning blind panic and anxiety.

Saturday afternoon an impromptu flight to Bilbao and by Sunday morning walking the Camino. He still says it saved him. I often consider the globalised stress of it all. A PFI industrial-style school, constructed by a French contractor with its profits tracked by a US management consultancy. Latin American cocaine, a pan-European aviation manufacturer running on a kerosene jet fuel pumped out of the ground of the Middle East.

And then an ancient Iberian pilgrim's trail. The only immutable truth in any of it.

SUNSET — RIBAMAR

ALONG THE CLIFF were a line of boyfriends, photographing girlfriends wearing dresses that matched the colour of the afternoon sky. They took a picture, and another picture, and then, another.

My hair caught on the wind.
My eyes are closed in it.
One more.
I look strange in that one.

I notice that all of the cameras, which are of course also phones though seldom used for talking, are all vertical; portrait. And I recall that when I was younger, most, if not all, of the photos were horizontal; landscape. In a simple rotation of the wrist, this is also the perfect illustration of how we have changed; our focus went from landscape, which is almost by definition looking at the world, to portrait, which is almost by definition looking at ourselves.

Down on the sands, up from the reaches of the waves, where the beach was smoothed by an earlier tide, a child plays in the sand, pursued by his mother. A phone is stretched forward, capturing the beautiful wide eyes of his unsuspecting face; a picture of innocence, to be dispatched from this edge of Iberia to the servers of a Silicon Valley company that will display his face amongst the advertising placements they have sold this day.

The sun sinks into the sea. It is a sunset sky, all blue and burnt oranges; a sky cloudless but for a single short, flat line of cirrus, winding in pink, and as if penned there, an autograph, like a signature to confirm another day done. Or a painter, signing a masterpiece.

TO BARCELONA

IN THE END I KNOW that I will have to take leave
of the Atlantic. There are moments, particularly as it rages,
gloomily, when it reminds me all too much this autumn of the
pandemic; vast, all-powerful, beyond our control. The ocean
is the opening to that same infinity, one that conspires to make
us feel so almost unbearably small.

Inland I turn, towards where Portugal becomes a land
of valleys and of hills, with the remnants of cloud and mist
and sometimes woodsmoke nestled between each fold,
crowned by a copse or small woodland. The villages stand in
patches of terracotta tile amongst the green; walls all painted
white. If this patchwork has about it any consistent hallmark,
then it is one of cultivation; of humans settling, building,
farming; able to make a life for themselves in the bosom of
nature, where its most extreme tempers have been tamed.
Into that sense of a greater comfort, leaning rightwards, I
turn with Miles, and together we move off the coast, and
into the interior.

With that right-hand turn, the mood changes, all of it anew. An old vine grows out of the garden and over the stone wall, throwing a final few cherry tomatoes, puckering dry and red, into the road. In the field are the hardened husks of abandoned pumpkins, the flesh all gone and only the small, humped pile of carapaces remaining. On a fig tree are the last fruits, burst dry and open so that now wasps hover over pink insides, and the rest of the season's yield is only a leathery skin; a natural bitumen pasted on the road below.

It is noticeable how suddenly all the land is different, how suddenly all the land is used.

Every divot and every hillock seems to have been cultivated or ploughed. Grape vines grow, leaf veins reddening with autumn. Small clearings of trees go felled and wood stacks pile high with the fuel for many villages. A man pushes his rotavator through the soil. In another field, the plough arm of a small tractor cuts fallow earth, green with weeds and grass, and as the engine opens and wheels turn, the blade simultaneously cuts and volts the earth up and over into richest, fertile blacks and browns.

Here the land is worked; sustaining life and livings, while on the coast merely the splendour of sea and sunset is milked, and locals instead aim to divert capital from the world's capitals to those who live beside the ocean. The coast is leisure, the interior is labour. Even the dogs work. Small little things with large, pointed ears, ever-alert, evolved to listen for rats or other rodents. Or cyclists, as always. With ratty little barks of their own, they scramble towards me until they meet the fence and bare tiny teeth. A larger dog runs the length of a garden to get at me, its bark coming to an abrupt halt only with the crashing of metal as it collides with the panel of the gate. I smile, schadenfreude.

Beside a bus stop with a water fountain and tap, I stop, noticing a tiled pattern and painting on the font, and the name, Fatima; Mohammed's daughter. Another piece of Islam left behind in this land now apparently Christian.

Across the road and beneath an apple tree sits a man in a wheelchair. His speech is slow and a little laboured, his hand moves as he speaks and his arm then lifts up high into a broad wave of greeting. He gives a toothless smile, and the words Onde Vai?! are called across the road between us.

It is a good question. Where do I go? I think about it, not yet sure, and little shared language will sustain this exchange, so that after a pause I say it: To Barcelona! And he replies, with a smile and a disbelieving shake of the head, Barcelona?!

I nod and I smile back.

I guess I'm going to Barcelona.

INTERIOR

EAST OF TEJO

THE LAND IN AN INSTANT is changed again. I look back, west of Tejo, at the crumpled masses of stone and crag and hill, where a force once pulled and rock ruptured into so many folds and rising elevations. East of Tejo, where I am headed, is flat. A perfect floodplain, somehow calming, all smoothed and reaching out to the horizon. The two land forms look askance at one another, as if acrimonious exes who can scarcely believe they were ever together. Only Tejo now connects them, water to earth, and at the same time holding them apart.

Across the river I pedal, looking south to the lights of Lisbon in orange, all up the hills and small cliffs of stone. There are the lights, parallel and flat to the water, marking a line of viaduct that must be a section of the vast Vasco da Gama Bridge, crossing Tejo. Below me the waters churn in that familiar way; the cogs of an intricate clock, with each eddy and undercurrent interlocking perfectly and bank-to-bank on this antique timepiece. Above me stand the wrought iron arches of the bridge, bolted fast, all so unglamorous and yet somehow attractive in its simple strength, with a deep sense of permanence to it. I consider my other great rivers and where I crossed them; Mississippi at Natchez; Yangtze at Nanjing. Hudson from George Washington Bridge, so many times. Danube, which I rarely crossed – maybe only once, at Ruse, Bulgaria – but often followed, as it widened and then gaped at the Black Sea. Perhaps a favourite was the less known Columbia, out through Oregon and glistening in the chandelier of first sun, emptying into Pacific.

For now though; other concerns. Already the dusk fades to dark; the moon is a perfect crescent, lying lazy and yellow on its back so that it gives no light, and will not for a few days more.

It is an iron law that sleeping in a spot you have not seen in the daylight is always more unsettling, and deciding on it still harder. The light is not so low that I do not see, accentuated in headlights, the dead form of a squashed viper. I imagine these Tejo floodplains; the rats that live in dens built in muddy banks between fields. The snakes that hunt the rats. The mosquitoes that hatch by the billion and wait for my face and neck. The dogs that were put-out. Make no mistake, here is not good camping.

Here is close to the wealth of Lisbon, though not close enough to share that wealth. Here is transitory, where workers and families are churned by employment no different to the eddying waters of the river. Here is the city's warehousing, and the factories that belong to the offices in Lisbon. Worse, many of the factories have moved elsewhere; to Asia, or maybe further east in Europe, and so those here are now closed, into disrepair. Here are the unkempt gaps where society frays, just as the iron holding doors rust and weeds grow up through broken glass. I know from experience that, in fact, here live the best of people, but I too, sadly, am a creature of the prejudices in which I habituate. At the other extreme, however, I also recognise that the perfect, zero-crime bourgeois little market town – where all the crime is committed quietly behind closed doors, but its streets are preserved so fair, with ivy growing down lamplit archways – looks welcoming but often isn't, because for the same reason it seems on the surface all zero-crime, my wayfaring soul is going to be hassled out of town post-haste.

Camping is always a mixture of absolutes and edges. Perfect, empty nature is of course ideal, with a few but not too many miles to the provisions of the next town for breakfast. Where you can't get such a thing, such as here, matters become harder. Sometimes, in lands like these, I like to sleep slightly closer to habitation, however undesirable, because the same activity of the habitation also deters animals – strays, pests, vipers – with the hubbub of a town to push them further from my bedside. There are humans in these places, but not too many. It is not the city nor the town. My security analysis is always, furthermore, that if I think one person can detect me in a place like this, it is better if a second person can detect me also. Should someone find me, I would like – just in case – for another person to be able to find them finding me. Underlying my final decision will be the conviction that sometimes it is better not to surprise people, go confident-like, as if sleeping here is the most natural thing in the world.

Nevertheless, privilege; I think of the black man hiking the Camino, of how both nature and the outdoors were made so white. Those who meet me will always meet a white person and react accordingly. I remember the young black man who once told me he'd stopped cycling, and camping in the fields where he pulled-up at a day's end, because the objections he encountered were so dispiriting. The greatest reservations I have encountered were farmers reminding me to take my empty wine bottle with me. Prejudices are lazy but have little need of rest; they occupy even the most open of spaces.

Aside from being discovered, there are considerations of weather. Among the agriculture I ride through are large trailers waiting, broad and solid, in roadside laybys. Their underneath looks like it would be dry, sheltered from any rain and hidden away. But I am never quite able to shake the fear of awaking to the trailer being hitched and wheels narrowly rolling either side of me. Sometimes there is a mosque, sometimes the yard of a church. Tonight, I will consider a fire station's grounds, perhaps the nearest secular thing to a building dedicated to saving souls, and staffed all night. I will pass the derelict barn beside the twenty-four hour petrol station; the perfect mix of shelter, privacy, but also a vetted staff member close at hand, but not too close. This staff member, it must be said, could help or hinder my efforts to camp, for the world's twenty-four hour petrol station workers, always divide neatly in two. One half are those who see opportunity in the fact that they're sitting there all night anyway, and watching-over me presents a rare and pleasant by-product to the otherwise monotonous shift. The other half understand their work precisely as the task of stopping me camping there.

I pull to the edge of the road, looking closer at this large barn beside the petrol station that has caught my eye. It looks perfect, but quickly I pass it up. This is based on a previously discovered logic: 'too perfect'. Here is a place others will also be drawn, as shown in the empty beer bottles and fire pits of the earth floor. Though I am homeless this night in precise status, I am not yet so in mind, and I do not want to meet and keep company in a ruined building on the edge of town at night.

Perhaps now, as I look for a resting place in these strange days of a pandemic, there is at least comfort in the idea that at least none of us have plans any longer. My nonconformity is for a while more conformist; an absence of plans has in relative terms grown more normal, more in-keeping with the rest of the Western world. Whatever the truth of that, more important right now is that nothing here will do for sleeping. And so on I ride…

…passing the silhouettes of large crop sprayers, their orbiting wheels and the bending arcs from which they are wrought and spread fifty metres, end-to-end of a field. The dust of dry earth rises in floodlights where a tractor is harrowing. A combine harvester across the road works late and under floodlights, so that I suppose such a large and expensive machine is rented a day at a time from those few farmers who own and drive them on behalf of the lessee, and so the days must be long. I pass a depot with a grape harvester waiting to return into the vines; the cab sitting high on top of tall tyres, and under it two twisting spirals that wind upwards and carry grapes into a hopper. Everything works late, and automatic gates on private roads roll shut behind large trucks making their way from silos back to the road. I hear the unmistakable cr-crack of gunshot, rifle fire, and then see two marksmen in wellington boots, side-by-side and weapons across their middle as they pace a field and leave me to wonder what they are shooting.

I make my peace with the road, resolved that on it I will stay a while in search of my night's home. The traffic is high, heavy; empty on my side of the road, but streaming on the other. Headlights, from the countryside, back to Villa Franca de Xira, to Lisbon. Out of them the smell of diesel, a chain of diesel, one engine after the next and lifting up. Some time ago I once looked at such a line of car traffic and briefly saw in it a train; only a train of infinite carriages, each one individually owned, maintained and driven in the exact same direction as all the others, peeling away for just the last few hundred metres of a journey to a front door, and each carriage with its own motor, decoupled by only a few metres in this five-hour long train. Since I first saw a line of cars in this way, it has proven very hard to un-see.

And so I ride east, beyond the Tejo, and the train of cars that could so easily have been a train goes west, back over it, and we make our different ways into the night.

BEUYS

CYCLING ACROSS IBERIA for no particular reason, and on a bicycle far worse than I should do it with, has about it, I like to think, that unswerving commitment to an idea, at once pointless but also strangely bewitching, that exists at the kernel of any true work of art.

Perhaps then this ride is also like a small work of art to me, like a painting or a quick sketch drawn in body and miles and map. It is not that what I am doing does not involve endeavour, for the pedalling has much of it, even too much. But it has little real purpose, and if something has too much purpose then it ceases to be art. If you try too hard to communicate something, a message or a feeling, then it cannot be art, it soon becomes activism. Here, I do nothing but pedal. I communicate only myself, from one point to the next. Sometimes I think the art the world needs most is that of behaviour without rational motivation, and that it need not be seen as art, but only a message for a different way of living.

Joseph Beuys, the old German artist, once created such a message. His friends collected him in New York, at JFK Airport, and they wrapped him in a blanket, blindfolded him, and then delivered him to an anonymous flat in rundown Manhattan, I think in the Bowery. There, they proceeded for a month to lock him in a room with a coyote, and a subscription to the Wall Street Journal.

No art will ever describe the United States so perfectly.

ALENTEJO WIND

THE WIND IN THE INTERIOR is not like that of the Atlantic that came before it. Where across the ocean it had pressed almighty and sometimes terrible, still it had been consistent, uninterrupted by the level plane of the sea it moved over. Inland it grew capricious, hostile; it would ricochet in and out of every ditch and culvert, hug the contours and then shoot forth, splitting either side of trees and fences and lonely water towers that here are all that mark the villages. Up and ahead you see it, crossing the road hand-in-hand with the dust clouds and, my word, but the dust.

It flies in from all sides, scattering a fistful of grit against your face, your eyes, any exposed skin. Dervishes of it spin down cart tracks. When you sit in cafés there is always a film of dust across every table and chair and ceramic surface; the saucer, the cup to the lips. At the table, opening a book to record these very words, soon it and I too are both specked with dust, with bits of old feather sticking to the wet nib of my pen.

Sometimes, vainly, it seems the wind might abate; that it is ready instead to rain. A few drops fall, but no more, as if they are too fast spirited away, pulled to wherever the wind will let them down. Here it will never rain. When, seldom, the dust desists, restoring invisibility to that wind, instead it picks up the smell of manure, spread across the fields, or, more often, up from around the animal troughs, lifted and thrown at me. For here is cattle country.

The herds have drunk the earth dry. Occasionally there is a green field; one, just one pasture surrounded by other parcels of land in greys and yellows. In the heart of it is an irrigation pipe, a hydrant, and then the cattle grazing; heads down and pure white longhorns up. At the roadside I see acorns, often just clusters of their empty cases, like a collection of downed goblets on the driest of banquet tables. Trees give their fruit to this painting; first quince and then olives and pomegranate. Sacks of oranges from the early season now passing are piled up beside the bins of a farmhouse. From off to one side, I see a pack of barking dogs pursuing an old and beaten-up car down a dusty cart track leading to a trailer.

Sometimes it feels like I have been here before. Sometimes here I am in central California; in an economically depressed interior beside an affluent coast. I ride on, I pass the same pampas grasses and then finally even the fragrant pepper trees that once I saw fruit pink peppercorns in California's wide San Joaquin valley.

And then I consider, why would it be any different? Portugal and California share a similar latitude, climates; similar ocean coasts that first harboured trade, and then the metropolises and new development that followed the trade. Both interiors hold agricultural hinterlands in a world less and less favourable to agriculture. The similarity of the Portuguese and Californian interiors comes as a reminder that all politics, really, is just geography. Portugal's interior is California's central valley is Portugal's interior. Both occur on identically corresponding parts of the globe, and the fact that one is called Portugal and the other California is due only to a complex labelling system in a filing cabinet of nations we created because we could not cope with our similarity as beings, nor the notion of our fair access to the world. Portugal and California, I realise as I ride, are only our different names for the same place.

In time, a new roadside appears, and I come to the forests of the Iberian cork trees. Their lowermost trunks and spreading branches are stripped; bark cut back to a wood rich red brown and bare, like trees dressed in red stockings up to their thighs, numbered and marked for harvest. In the cross-section where the bark resumes, you see the yellow, fleshy wood, waiting to close wine bottles and provide sandal soles and gentrified flooring solutions across the continent. I marvel to think that once, in simpler times, this bark was harvested to make the helmets of racing car drivers, and each of these uses has sustained these trees, their farmers, and the peculiar ecosystem where finches bob across the land and into trees. At my feet go lines of ants, all but invisible, carrying grains of corn thrice their size in jaws before them, back towards their nests, so that all I see are the moving grains, and a perforated, dotted line across the earth.

On the edge of a small village, I near two middle-aged women; custodians to this crop and who load large bundles of neatly-cut cork strips into the boot of a car. Before I see this sight, however, first I smell the women; each perfectly perfumed. I see them in their neat silver perms and blazers with gold buttons. One tightens twine around the next bundle, as the other woman handles the last into the small boot of the small car nearing capacity. And I smile as I pass, still breathing in the last of their perfume. Why was this scene so perfect? I try to unravel what made it such a delight. And though it is often a curse to put beauty into words, I think, pedalling on and after a while, I think it is because the sight and smell of them while hard at work disproves simultaneously the ideas that femininity is not hardy, and that labour is not elegant.

At a bend in the road, up ahead, gathered at a mound of earth beneath a concrete pylon: a herd of horses, the largest of them jet black and with a shining mane that flashes in this grey and brooding landscape. The animal is perched like a king, atop his mound, the mane flicking as if a spark of flint against the grey sky. In one strong motion, he turns his head to look at me and this bicycle. I look back at the gathering of tails, the bulging haunches, long heads all so perfect and serene, standing in the dusty yellow grass, framed beneath the concrete right-angles of the pylon. A lone brown horse gallops

a little way distant, against the gathering storm. On the barbs
of a barbed wire fence, shards of black plastic are caught, tear,
flapping against the storm. Higher up, at the top of the pylon
are tiny wind turbines, like weather vanes with small egg cups
filling constantly with the wind, spinning on unoiled axles that
shriek and whistle as they each feed a little more electricity
into the cables. The wires hum above the gathered horses, and
in the meeting of the two – of man and nature, of chaos and
harmony – there is somehow an image that explains it all. A
painting for all time.

And all the while, the wind ripped through.

Far worse and more hostile than the wind was the traffic
and its drivers, some buffeted by the gusts as they slammed into
their sides and caught the metal sails on those tiny highway
boats. The interior is the sort of place where traffic includes
bulldozers and excavators on wide, flat trucks with flashing
lights above them and taking up two-thirds of the road. You
duck as they approach with the fistful of air they throw out
in exchange.

To ride is to know power, vulnerability, and the immutable
fact: car drivers are the worst. Down empty highways they
scream, rocking on their axles and careering forth with a
presumption that on the road ahead they will meet with nothing
but themselves. Sometimes they go swerving, late, away from the
cyclist oncoming; and other times they do not even trouble with
this much. The villages of the interior are the in-between places,

places from which control feels pulled away, lost towards the cities, and so the ability to floor an accelerator remains one final means by which a person might still feel a little power in their own life.

Alongside me, a few are on bicycles; beautifully old and rusting things but perfect for a couple of miles between home and work, home and school, home and home. The bicycles are ridden by those without financial means to buy cars, or with sense and spirit enough to realise they don't need to. On an old green thing with a basket, a large middle-aged woman pedals, wearing an apron to what must be a shift in a canteen somewhere. Her face is scowling in determination at an incline, her bicycle creaking as, instantly, she becomes a hero to me. An hour later, I watch her cycle back as still I wait, still in the café, still stared-at by each man getting from a van or truck. Walking in, looking at me. I nod or smile a greeting back at each of them; and they stare, as if whatever response they expected from me to their stare, it wasn't this.

RAINFALL — CAVALEIROS

I ARRIVE OUTSIDE THE CAFÉ, in a wide and dusty forecourt with a half dozen cars parked-up. I cough deeply, and though it is out of keeping with the times, discreet as I can, I must; spit. Men look at me, suspicious, but – pandemic or otherwise – I feel that theirs is only the time-honoured response to a stranger's arrival off of the road. Armed with only my look, apologetic, I aim to reassure them that this was only the last of the ocean's salt air, and the first of the interior's dust, coming up out of my lungs.

The sky is darkening still. The café is one of those where every customer is a man in overalls and the one woman in the place is the owner who holds complete authority over all of them.

On the opposite side of the road, a dog with three legs runs down the pavement and reminds me of the off-balance nature of Miles and his bent crank, only the way the animal moves is the more elegant and efficient. Next door, a Romani woman sweeps the patio of her house.

The clouds, the Atlantic. They heard my complacency, my innermost thoughts that these clouds could not rain. They sent forth. Four days of it, according to a man arriving across the threshold of the café porch, shaking his head of its droplets, calling out loud – "Quatro Dias!" – and holding up four fingers. He is smiling in that way humans sometimes do when they are caught in the rain, but caught only enough to make them inexplicably very happy, as if showing that in us is a great and mostly untapped tolerance for inconveniences so long as they at least remind us we are alive. Another man looks at me, also sheltering. He smiles, and shrugs his expression. What can you do?

Seated on the porch, I watch as its corrugated roof begins to trickle and then becomes a series of flumes. The wind remains, only now bringing in great garlands of raindrops that swirl and then burst in mid-air. Peow! The sky turns to white, we are in the cloud, the wave breaking. The rain goes trickling down the walls from a gap where the porch meets the building proper, but the roof otherwise holding fine. Not a drop. An alert, onto my phone. A public service message. 'Two days, high winds and rain. Take care.' It is written in Portuguese and English. I look up again at the sky, howling a confirmation of the message. Accurate.

This will be rain from an ocean. Will be rain like no other. This land the first thing this cloud has met for weeks. Rain that will keep you up at night; at first in a good way, enchanting, on the canvas of a tent or terracotta of tiles, but then in a way that will eventually come to seem unreasonable, that will just seem unfair, and like it might at any moment break into your home. From above, onto the plastic roof, the rain hammers, presses down, oppressive and without relent. No drop penetrates, but the sound, the sound is colossal.

In truth, that sound, it sounds like the world right now; each raindrop represents one problem, one life, and it lands all together and at the same time, in an irrepressible din that sits right over your ears and seems like it will never end. Perhaps it will end, in two days' time, or four, but in this crushing racket, such a length of time seems like its own eternity. I look at the bicycle, at Miles; droplets hanging on the frame, a snail climbing intrepid up the arc of the tyre. I remember that this right now is all my home, is all my possessions, is all that I have.

Travelling light is good. Mobility can be an eloquent solution to all manner of problems, but three days of rain is a problem unsuited to the solutions I'm working with. I get to my feet and walk to the woman at the bar. I order port. A different kind of solution.

In its small thimble of a wine glass the port arrives. She sets it down with a smile; like she is glad to take care of me, like I should settle in, make myself at home. A moment later she returns, inexplicably but all in tenderness; with a smile, she places down a gift. I look to the table, where the proffered little plastic parcel waits, shining. And, on closer inspection, she seems for some wonderful reason to have gifted me a small, red ceramic cockerel attached to a key ring. And with the port hitting just right, delighted, I look up at her, and together we beam into one another's faces.

I watch the raindrops come, shaking, as they crash into the surface of the puddles; like bricks through glass and disappearing into a dark world below, bringing all the energy of the sky down upon the earth. The bar fills up, everyone with the same idea, everyone ordering a drink, as if the rain has thrown an unexpected party for us all, obliging us to make friends in this temporary home of an afternoon together.

These, as I say, are the in-between places, and let me tell you that I would swap them for nothing, for I grew up in one of them, which in time leaves one with a loyalty to all of them, and an ability to recognise them all.

They are not quite suburbs; they are richer than that, precisely because they are poorer, but they share the commonality of falling outside of those places we deem to be of interest. They are places that push you out because, growing up, they seemed so terrible and limited, and you could make your peace with them, but only if, just once, something could just happen. But it doesn't. And so, instead, these places instil in you an ability to find interest, to entertain yourself and seek out whatever curiosity their world can offer. Finally, in the end they propel you out, with a magic of their own, even if that magic is simply a sense that there must be something more than this. Eventually you reach the larger places, but there you find mostly just pretension, and in time learn the lesson that life perhaps never got purer than that fear of a first kiss with a girl, while both drunk underage in a local recreation ground in dire need of investment.

These places can lack the refinements of the city, there is sometimes an ignorance of the outside world here which can manifest in anxiety, prejudice and rejection. But in truth, I have never been able to judge these things as a cardinal sin, for to do so would, I fear, be a more terminal condition than the ignorance itself, which in my view often melts with experience.

People round here, they don't change their minds so much as city folk, but when they do, their mind is changed. Perhaps it is simply so that a human must see new evidence a hundred times before normalising it, and in a city that number is met within a year, but here, perhaps a decade.

Sometimes this is the slower path to change, but it is the more enduring. Stubbornness, too, brings with it a safety, a protection against any change too fast. Through stubbornness the gains we make are eventually locked-in. A part of us embraces that which is new, a part of us insists on the old. If both parts speak back-and-forth, if both hold equal power, then each trait can have its function, and we remain connected. If there is friction in this process, it is often generated by imbalances of power rather than an underlying belief. Sometimes discord is greatest when everyone has limited power, when power has been taken from them, leaving people of all beliefs to grip harder at those small areas in which they can still feel some control.

A secret, quickly, as the port goes to my head and softens my guard. For all that I say this, for all that I believe it, the place where I grew up instilled in me a constant need to get out, to leave, and it took a long time to exhaust. I have always been escaping. Home and escape are inherently related, opposing but bonded ideas; you escape into the world to get out of a home, or you find a home in which you escape the world. Sometimes, you have a home so difficult it makes you crave the world and its roulette wheel; the idea that any other number you land on will be better. Other times the world tires you so that, as you go rattling round its wheel, any home becomes preferable.

Outside the bar a man appears, gets out from a car to the forecourt; he is perhaps gypsy, perhaps Arab. He sings quietly to himself, in a low honey voice and a language neither Arabic nor Portuguese, as he reaches for and lights a cigarette. And he alone of the arriving men gives a smile as he sees me, and I smile back at him and this music in his soul. As if born to perform, he notes my approval, he lets the music play, takes the cigarette from his mouth and the volume of his lungs lifts up into song. These, I think, are the gems, uncut, that you find in the in-between and which make all life worth living. There is more purity in them than any concert hall, auditorium, conservatoire or gallery. He performs only for his soul's own joy, and any audience is – as audiences should be – an afterthought.

BREAK IN THE CLOUDS

IT SEEMED THERE WAS a halt in the rain, and perhaps it was one of those opportunities that we seize only to find it was an illusion; it had briefly existed but just as quick was gone.

Or perhaps that break in the cloud was a stationary one, and so I cycle out of its nurturing dry portal and back under the raining sky.

Soon I am wet; though still dry enough to feel myself getting wet, and so I try to resist it. Both the sensation of the wet and the resistance to it are a curse all of their own. In ten minutes I will actually be wet and all the better for it. Out of this present purgatory, I will dampen and then soak, and with the temperature still mild, I might, if I am lucky, be let into that euphoria that is riding in the rain.

Miles, below me, seems almost agreeable. I notice him running quieter, the rain a temporary lubricant that will then leave his joints and rivets drier and creaking all the more. I take a back route, signposted for the next town, but the road leading off of the main highway. The road runs up and down each rise; one of those rural roads made from giant slabs of concrete, placed down on earth and now cracking apart under their own weight, the weight of vehicles heavier than mine. The fractured slabs press down into the mud, squeezing up around it. The concrete swaps with cobbled sections, then back to concrete, then cobbles again, with pools of water where a cobblestone is missing. Soon the road is pulling all hope of momentum out of a bicycle that struggles with momentum at the best of times.

On the right, the cork trees come to an end, with the rain running red down the wood beneath the bark. Cork gives way to a small plantation of eucalyptus; the aroma lifting in moist air and that smell of a childhood balm rubbed by a mother on to a back; this scent a small piece of the world's magic, my mood changing with it. Up ahead the hill picks higher; I crank a little at the pedals, rain into my eyes and mouth moving back to a smile. I cannot see over the hill but each metre my wheels climb higher up it, bringing me head-height to the summit. And there it is.

A valley opens in front of me, perfectly full with the ruddy yellow of harvested wheat, glowing bright in what last light the sky can offer. The road is rutted but glistening silver in the rain, and shoots straight across to a far hillside; this patchwork of yellow and silver framed all around by a woodland of purest green. I roll into the valley, flooding in on its silver road, and I see the chaff of the wheat pierce yellow from the silt-grey mud of the river basin. My silver road leads me onto a narrow concrete bridge, elevated up, where either narrow side of me grow flowering lilies across small ponds that fill before my eyes with muddy waters and the rain. Another flooded field of chaff and silt begins in blacks, greys and yellows, though all through this new field stride dozens and dozens of storks, their white feathers slick and legs picking in and out the furrows of water. Beaks long and pink now and then go nodding down into a pool as the storks walk on stilts across the scene.

A bird sees me; heads turn, a few take flight while others walk on, nonchalant as, in the rain, I smile; I smile full.

Out of nowhere, over the next rise, the world is waiting. It did it again, it always will. This is the lesson.

CORUCHE

THE NIGHT IS DEEP, for a while the sky has run dry above where I shelter, beneath a lean-to at the side of the road. For hours I consider whether to stay until dawn, but eventually I pack up and return to riding. Sleep does not come for me anyway, and in the morning it will be raining again. These ten miles to the next town will feel longer in the rain. For now the sky is clear, and anyway, I always loved the nighttimes, when it feels like you're the only one left.

Ahead of me the heat of long summer is still locked in the road, so that I see its steam winding upwards, in that familiar way, as rainfall cools asphalt. In the shaft of my head torch light, the steam moves, so too the occasional droplets of drizzle, darting for me on the wind. Now and then a moth comes towards me and my single bar of light. The bats cut their arcs and white lines of the road lean away into each bend. In the trees at the roadside I smell pine, and eucalyptus again returns. Logging trails have all across the afternoon turned to rivers, so drifts of sand and silt have emptied across the road. A cat is crouched, eats the roadkill guts of a squashed animal; a frog, I think. Cat's eyes on me as I pass.

I feel my rhythm getting up, then red lights flash ahead and a bell rings as barriers lower across me. The red shimmers on the wet, and loud and crashing there comes the sound of an engine nearing the level crossing. Quickly it steals through, just one cart; a maintenance carriage, a hopper on wheels and with a shoot, perhaps to lay the stones that the sleepers will rest upon.

For a long time the barriers stay down, bells ringing way beyond the time when it appears safe to go again. Once I would have stolen under, but now I am older; more cautious, more obedient, both? And so I wait. Soon after the train tracks, the town comes: Coruche, a town like many others.

It is still deep in the early hours, sky jet black but still rainless. I would like to rest a little, but somewhere dry. The gates to the church are shut fast. I roll down a street; I see a deep-set doorway, totally concealed, but a shadow in it as I roll past. I double-back, just to check; not to look close, I don't want to disturb anyone, but yes, sure enough; a man sits-up in there, his shadow looking at me. He needs that doorway more than I do.

Out to the other side of the town centre I roll, following the River Sorraia, which could either be chance, or come from the Farsi word, Soraya, by which Iranians refer to a constellation of stars, and is the Arabic for a galaxy.

Eventually my road stops before a large imposing circle; an arena, gates all round it and I realise that, yes, here is the bull ring; empty of its crowds and beasts. Beside it is a small structure of many bays, open, but like a stable and beneath a pitched roof of tiles. Against its frame I sit, the smell of hay coming over to me from the ring, and I lower the peak of my cycling cap down over my eyes, only to be disturbed by a scuttling, out of the corner of my eyes; small but larger than anything I can think likely. The scuttling is no rodent, but then it is no bug or insect either.

I get up, step towards it, and then under armour and behind claws, yes, but surely not? Walking down the street, a hundred miles from the sea, a crab arches up and bares its pliers, unperturbed by my size. I back away, return to my rest; chin on chest, cap over eyes, as a small street-sweeping cart rounds the corner and, all headlights and fluorescent nylon rotating brooms, drives right by where the crab just so bravely made its last stand.

And I suppose this is how we humans destroy the world; not in conscious evil, but unthinking and banal. So it goes.

Behind the street cart a worker follows, dressed in fluorescent trousers and with a municipal cap on top of another perfect perm. She holds a twig brush and sweeps the pavements into the gutter for the cart to hoover up. She sees me, sitting on the floor, and gives a look of disapproval, but an ambiguous one. If she is judging me then it is neither stern nor personal. She looks simply as if I am a sorry sight to see, with an edge of 'what is this town coming to?' and perhaps also, 'it didn't used to be like this. How things change.'

As the sky pales, looking out at the street, I watch as the row of city lights along the promenade turn off. Instinctively I smile, for I find a small magic in this moment, when night officially becomes day in the eyes of the town, and just for a second I am in on this twice-daily secret of its running order.

I roll back through to the centre, finally find my quarry; the first open café, run by the man who rises early and knows how much he can make if he opens before the competition. Outside a customer is just leaving, finishing an espresso on a wine barrel table. Pools of warm yellow light fall from inside, and I pull on my mask and enter through a fly net over the doorway.

The proprietor rests in a corner, looks exhausted, worse than me; perhaps not an early riser after all. His face is behind a mask, eyes look to be still beneath his duvet. In his chair he sits, splayed; legs spread, arms back, one limb of his own pointing with each chair leg down into the floor. He sees me and peels out of it, heaving up on the arm like it's the rope of a boxing ring in round twelve. He steps behind the counter, arms spread across it, now a broker at the bourse. He turns to his coffee machine, sets it off, hammering, with my order, then pulls out a cinnamon shaker and businesslike places it on the counter alongside my nata. Outside I sit, coffee and nata, as a heavy church bell clangs and there nears the familiar sound of the street-sweeping cart, and up from a narrow lane comes my sweeping woman and her twig broom. She sees me, up from the street and now served with my own coffee and nata; a regular customer, like I've turned out OK, did all right for myself, better than she'd hoped. Like the system works after all.

I sit, I watch the town as the cart passes through and the street quietens again, before the world awakes. Two children with schoolbags cross the main square, laughing. Overhead, against a sky lightening to pink, there flies a small flock of birds, finches, and they move in formation; together then apart, together then apart, contracting–expanding–contracting so that, for only a second, it is as if I am watching a heartbeat go flying through the air.

RAINBOWS — ESTREMOZ

THE SKY ITSELF is always the first thing to stop raining. After it the roof tiles continue to rain, the leaves for a while continue to rain, and last and longest of all, the gutters will continue to rain.

When finally it stops raining in the Alentejo, soon it is unbelievable to think that ever it rained at all. For a moment, in the last of the rain, the trees glisten a bright emerald in the returning sun, but then the moisture passes and the leaves simply shine white. The sandy earth drains quickly dry. The water winds in steam up from the hot land, a rainbow is come, then gone, and the ivory of the longhorn cattle flash as they lift from the ground, kept dry beneath them, and they stand and watch you.

Soon you are hot again, and water from the sky, even a little, would be some great miracle.

As I laboriously push Miles forwards, through flooded olive groves that now reflect sheer, shining blue sky, still we are making progress. I see trucks with canvases marked with the names of companies that own them; fruiterers, fabricators. I see the location of their business: the city of Badajoz, which I know awaits. I see an Italian number plate upon a truck, and I can feel Europe starting, like I am leaving its very edge and venturing inwards towards its heart.

The trucks drive sometimes in close formation, one slipstreaming the other, taking it in turns to share the improved fuel economy of the draft, no different to cyclists in a peloton. I see sheep at the roadside, some lambs, one sheep with its head stuck in a wire fence, dispensing life advice by determinedly making the most of a bad situation; devouring the longer grass the other side of the fence, like it will trouble with the future only when it comes.

Whereas I have often found myself on Rua Lisboa, now I find a first Rua Valencia. It is always so sweet, those first tell-tale signs where the geography signals the way you plan to go, and you get the first indications that, perhaps, you might make it.

Down the street, getting up from the table at a café, an old man begins the walk home. His pace suggests that he does not have far to go. His feet barely lift from the floor, his movement a shuffle forwards with the perfect efficiency of minimal effort. He places his hands behind his back; one hand holds the wrist of the other arm, in that way men of a certain age eventually begin to, all over the world. It is as if he is inspecting troops, inspecting the world, or at least, he is inspecting his world.

This evening, when I finish my day's riding, above the spot where I will sleep, I do the same. Just for a few paces, I practise being older. One of the joys of travel on a bicycle, living at the roadside, is the raw simplicity. So that an evening activity, the thing that fills your mind, can be as simple as how you stand. Just you and the world.

And so I survey my world. And it feels good. My hand takes my other arm at the wrist and pulls it across to it, just like the old man, which I realise in turn has pulled my shoulders back and so opens my chest, making more room for my lungs. I feel like I breathe a little deeper. And I think that maybe I could get used to standing like this, and that so many men, in so many countries all around the world, cannot be wrong.

ORANGES AT VEIROS

LIKE BAUBLES THEY HANG in the tree, wet with mist and the most recent spell of that rain, the drizzle that keeps in and out. Most are still green, some blush their final colour. Others have turned most of that orange and so now appear to blush green. Others still are too far gone; either dropped to the road, or on the tree but splitting open, with the fruit darkening black as it bursts the skin.

A few seem all the way there; ripe. I pick one, a little hesitant, for some oranges can look the part but should never be eaten. Too sharp, too tart; non-edible varieties to begin with. I pick one down that is most all of orange in colour, I put my blade to it and the knife slices effortlessly in. I cut out a quarter, which smiles at me; a semi-circle in my hand.

The fruit inside looks like a heart dissected; that first bulb from which an orange grows, now cut open, revealed in cross-section like a tiny, plump aorta. Each triumphant parcel of fruit is now cut through, glistening, and if aesthetic perfection is any clue to taste, but this will be delicious. Into my mouth I place my quarter, smile a wide orange rind mouth to any car that passes on the empty road. I have my moment, to myself; that moment which the world now so often denies us, almost to a point at which, lost in the sea of moving time, a moment ceases to exist.

The juice flows. And it is good. It is good. Chilled by the cool of night, sweetened by the summer, pure orange juice bursts out of the skin and down my throat with the sting of citrus, a tearing of flesh as I bite the fruit and it comes away so agreeably, like it too wanted this to happen. In this moment, I have everything; have all that I could ask for. I savour the taste, the juice, the sharp vitamins and their sense of health. I stand on this winding hillside and savour the accidents of the universe that saw a tree grow here in this spot and commanded the orange to be a fruit so supreme.

Fruit picked fresh and free and from the roadside always tastes better. It has about it the bonus of costing nothing, the simple miracle of food, and the added flavour of growing slow and at nature's pace. This is true of all fruits; of all the apples, figs, berries and pears. But I'm not sure, standing here at the roadside in Portugal, that there is ever a found fruit that can compete with an orange.

And then I think of the Turkish word for an orange, which suddenly makes a fuller sense to me: Portakal.

SPAIN

EXTREMADURA

BADAJOZ

I CAME THIS WAY once before. A long time ago now.

In some ways it started in Badajoz. Badajoz was the first night alone as I cycled from the UK to Lisbon, having parted that morning from a friend I'd grown up with and who I'd cycled with as far as Bilbao. Bilbao to Lisbon had that morning felt far, and so I immediately caught a bus; two hundred miles east. To Salamanca. When the bus pulled in to Salamanca, Lisbon still felt far, and so I quietly missed my stop, stayed on one more, to Cáceres. End of the line. In Cáceres I got out. 80 kilometres and it was Badajoz.

I rode straight out. I wanted to arrive, wanted to be there, there in Lisbon. I wanted the destination and not the journey. I put in what I could before nightfall, rode into what felt like desert. I remember I was afraid of scorpions, despite not being sure if there were even scorpions in Spain. But that's not the point of fear – it knows no reason. I climbed off the road, but only so far as a rocky ditch just below the level of the road. I didn't want to go further and risk scorpions. I knew I was being irrational – of course there were also the poisonous spiders to consider, and then snakes, many of them, all writhing in my mind, and so why was I so scared of scorpions? I felt that the nearby road, and the vibration and noise of its traffic, would have scared away the scorpions. In that much I was right, though I still remember the shard of rock I had for a pillow. I still remember the white screaming headlights and noise of each passing car on the bend above. I didn't sleep well that night.

This time it's easier. Here is that familiar crossing point, the grey area. I pass the border in its traditional mixture of failed business, overgrown gardens, freight and human vice. Gambling, cheap perfume, the seedier stuff is out of sight in broad daylight, but it'll be around, waiting later and under shining neon light for a lonely truck driver.

On the route down into town are families, where I haven't seen families for a while. Only old people. I see a woman in a hijab with a pushchair, and realise that this makes me feel a little at home, in a way I'd never have expected. I follow the road up into town and I cross the river. I sit beneath the cathedral, where a beggar makes his way around its wall, leaning on a crutch, like nothing has changed in half a millennia save for the invention of the alloy and the rubber stopper where the crutch would once have been wood. Above, the bell tolls, reassuring with the weight of centuries through which it has always done that, and only that. I see the bell from the underside in copper green, streaked. Street cats chase one another across the main square and up cathedral steps.

A group of young poets are meeting at the next table in the main square; trench coats, leather caps, cigarettes, always being rolled and relit. A woman sees me take out pen and paper and begin writing. She reaches over and shows me her own; but her English is thin and my Spanish thinner, and so our contact is no more than this public intimacy of showing each other our words, the words we wrote, meaningless as they are to one another. I suppose it is nice only to know that they exist – a sort of naked picture, a part of one another we will never otherwise see, and would not have shared so lightly if we also shared a language, and could fully understand the glyphs of the other. Our incomprehension keeps us hidden.

They drink, they sit a while. One boy begins to recite a work; more a rap than poem, fast paced and I only really catch the last line, into which he slows for impact, as if here the verse bursts:

Miasma y pandemonium son hermano y hermana
Y tú lo sabes.

And I think I get:

Miasma and pandemonium are brother and sister
And you know it.

They all applaud. The girl takes her turn. On the opposite side of the square, buskers strike up; a cellist and flautist, the flautist dancing to his own tune and all the young poets exploding like bombs.

Night comes down, the belfry of the cathedral glows in white, a moon all of its own. I do not know where I plan to sleep, but – having returned to the scene of my first fear – I am not afraid. Perhaps crossing the river to look around, seeing Badajoz itself, it put something to bed, taught its lesson.

There are no scorpions.

LAUGHTER – DEEP SPAIN

HERE IS WATER TOWER COUNTRY. Emptiness but for more livestock and its yellowed grassland. The village sits a little way off the highway, itself only a circle of houses connected by a small feeder road. The bar is busy; Saturday afternoon, men outside, drinking but all silent. They keep only the company of their beer. One man says something as I pull up on my bicycle. There is a cackle of laughter at this joke that I suspect was at me and not with me. I look up at all the laughing faces, which are harmless but unfriendly. And yet, in the heart of the cackle, I sense that fraction-second of uncertainty when each man tries to figure out when to stop laughing. The image in front of me is the strength of a tribe meeting the fragility of its individual members.

Together, the men falter.

No-one wants to be either the first or the last to stop, and since the joke was not funny to begin with there is no organic point at which the laughter should end. The only joke was that they were the group and I wasn't, and now that has already been established, there is little more to it.

If you could map and isolate this moment, where tribe meets individual and inclusion meets exclusion, then waiting there would you find a truth that unlocks all marketing and politics, and vast riches, and great and almighty power would unfurl before you.

Often I have seen this moment, but I do not understand how and why it forms; not yet.

MOONRISE

EVERYTHING SHIFTS. I suppose that I have moved inland and away from the warmth of the Gulf Stream. And so the weather is colder here, as night falls and the sun vanishes. A chill lifts up from out the rivers and serrated lakes, cut like feathers, that rest hidden within these hills.

Winter nears. I aim to ride later, changing my day to break late in the afternoon, then ride out all of the daylight, squeeze every last drop of light from my sky. At around seven the sun is set and, just as last year and next, it will slip away about two-and-something minutes earlier each day. Every day I watch it disappear to the internal words: 'don't go.'

Then, I eat; then, I ride. I ride the night, shortening the hours of darkness where I lie in a sleeping bag that in all honesty is too thin, and in which the chill jaws of the mist come for me hard, biting first at my feet and then further up my legs. I will sleep on my front, arms folded under me to keep my chest off the cold, cold ground.

The moon, however, is also rising, making the night with its quiet roads almost kind to ride. When winter comes, and the sun sets too early, it is always in such a time that you learn to love the beauty of the moon.

A sense of pressure is also growing. The Spanish state of emergency is now two days old. It is more relaxed than its immediate, frantic opening on Monday morning, when a man in an empty and spacious street snapped at me for not having a mask on. Always is the fear of more to come, and with little warning. Up ahead, EU Schengen rules dictate that French borders must remain open, but I will not be permitted to leave a house in France without documentation authorising my movement. I have neither such documentation nor a house in France, so that decides it.

The boats, from Galicia to Devon, still sail, though not for foot or bicycle passengers, who eat into the boat's permitted passenger capacity while offering less fare than the cars and trucks. Perhaps in Barcelona I will get what price I can for Miles and then fly straight out. The idea has its appeal. But I don't like flying, and fly where?

At times, the mood of the pandemic compounds the uncertainty in my movement, while shutting out some of its joy.

Tonight will be a full moon, and I plan to ride my way into the last five hundred kilometres to Barcelona. I think it can be done.

The moon rises, yellow and enormous against the mountains, proving, as it lifts, the immutable law that when you see a full moon, the first face you think of is the one you love.

CONEJO

AFTER DUSK I STOP FOR FOOD, a truck stop beside a motorway exit. I watch the journeys from the bridge above the road, the headlights through the dark. Each of them looks to have such a sense of purpose, of necessity, destiny – kismet, or kader as it's also known in Turkish – as if all of these journeys had to happen and are important, which I suppose they must be, because they would otherwise have been cancelled. In the same way, when I now see people together, it is as if I am witnessing something tender and special, by virtue of the mere fact that they are there, together.

A twenty-four hour restaurant with floodlit forecourt. Inside is full of wood smoke, turning like a Catholic mass, where it winds up from a large hearth with an open fire and grill on it, and where the logs inside collapse to embers. Everyone wears a mask, with the exception of one traffic cop who strides through to the toilet with his mouth wide open and gun on hip. Cops: all the same.

I sit out front in the last of the half-light. Across the road are a small family of black pigs; two adults and many piglets, some of the relatives of which I'm sure have previously crossed the road to this grill. There is a set menu, with many words I don't understand, and then conejo, which judging by the roadside warrens was also once local, and so, I think, a meat with less environmental impact. We tell ourselves what we want to hear. When it arrives, cooked tender, salty, charred and perfect, I give a small prayer of gratitude and apology to all those little rabbits – adorable – with which I shared the last hundred kilometres of highway.

From my table, alone, I watch the highway. The motorway is ongoing. The unmistakable thump of truck axles entering a bridge section; the wind; the whine of an engine heading into night. The lights on the rigs, always, those lights on the rigs. Trucks always when I looked at them held an air of something between sacrifice and service, especially at night. I remember Jose Mari, a long time ago and the first trucker I ever rode with. He was from Extremadura, but picked me up on a Catalan roadside, hitchhiking. I remember, as we talked, he knocked down a sun visor to show there a picture of a young girl; ponytail, school dress, smiling. Daughter. And by chance, that day was her birthday. Eight years old. And then Jose Mari sort of threw up his hands from the wheel. And I'm here! Truckers – all those fathers, husbands and sons. A crummy way to earn a living, but at least a living.

On and under the bridge opposite, two trucks cross; one above and one below, forming a cross-stitch of white and orange light in the dark. The cargo constructs the world, quietly, even now. Each one is like seeing trade take place, a kind of signal of intent. Beside me a truck rolls out of the forecourt, driver leaning forward with both forearms resting over the top of the wheel. He yawns large and, in the privacy of his own cab, has no interest in stifling it with a hand. One day soon a satellite will control this cab, empty down the highway, and this man will yawn elsewhere; in a life set free of work, or condemned to precarity. Collectively, we will choose.

At the next table, I watch one man finish three beers then head for his van, his face weary as he shifts into the driver's seat. I feel a similar tiredness coming at me after my meal, but I must keep moving, as if the pandemic has become a small engine all of its own, and which demands either resolution or motion.

To move is the only power I am left with, and so I move.

The country rolls ahead, opening up. Moonlight gleams in the giant fermentation tanks that mark the vineyards and their wineries. Cows scream, or cry, in a vast dairy. The orange lights of a road crew roll on the hill ahead. A small village is shut-up, everything dark but one building illuminated. I look over at it; a manchego vendor. The building is a low set, floodlit thing with pictures and words about manchego painted on the walls. Serving suggestions are illustrated; manchego with grapes, manchego with a bottle of wine, just manchego on a wooden board. Despite the pictures, the building looks sinister, a bit like an old county gaol. It has railings over its only window, and a heavy door is strapped and bolted with iron braces, as if the cheese has had to be locked away for everyone's safety, the stuff so strong it might attempt a jailbreak. That manchego, a real bad motherfucker.

When finally I stop, taking my rest beside an olive tree in a newly-ploughed grove, I listen to the sound of the dogs barking; wild and feral and seemingly everywhere. I will eventually on this ride become a more careful listener to these barks, so relevant have they now grown. I will aim to discern if the bark is moving or if it remains at the same location. Tethered. This is my own rudimentary human sonar. Is it a restrained barking, repetitive, so that you can tell it is on a leash, tied to a stake? Or is the bark roaming free?

Disbelieving, I ask myself if all this was once just background noise to me? Is this just Iberia, with its hunting culture and its hounds?

Am I less brave, or are there more dogs?

And then again, looming towards me each time, the other option: now, unlike then, I am simply afraid. I got the fear.

MAINTENANCE

MILES IS NEVER QUIET, still less silent, which means there is never any silence when I am together with Miles. Which is always. Sometimes I try to humorise, to humanise, the failing. The keys of Miles' trumpet need oiling. Miles has a new sound, a new noise. I like to imagine him telling Duke Ellington about this new sound he's found, how there is nothing good in it.

Sometimes it annoys me too much for the effort of imagination or of mirth. Sometimes, lying there all peaceful and first thing in the morning, I look at Miles and I don't want to ride because it means I'll have to hear that noise again.

Other times I look at him, propped-up, like we both know that if he breaks, gives out, then that's it. I'll be on the next train and he'll never see Barcelona. There is no shame in that. Don't believe the adverts; sometimes, quitting is a great skill to master. Finding quests where there is no need of one is a hindrance to a life well lived. My friend; you already proved yourself. Do not be burdened, for no good ever came of it.

The thing is, though, I know the life I took Miles from, and that he'd never have lived this life without me.

And secretly, I suspect he too wants to see the streets of Barcelona. And so he'll make it.

FIDDLER RETURNS

I FOLLOW A WINDING TRAIL of gravel and pebble, with a ford crossing the road ahead. My shadow, impatient, shoots ahead of me as I near the ford, and there in the shallows are familiar creatures. The sun is on them this time, so clearly a shade of bright red compared to the previous and matt grey shape of Coruche at dawn. Here, again, are the freshwater crabs, the fiddler crabs.

I look down at one of them, its eyes looking back at me, front-centre in its head, shining bright blue. The thing rears up at me, puts up a show of strength just the same as last time; pincers high and brave. But as I look down, right away the crab retreats, backs slowly off and changes course. The eyes are fixed upon me so clear I almost see fear in them, in the tiny dots of a pupil. I see life washing before the thing – the stones and pebbles of the riverbed, the cool water over its shell beside mother crab – and quickly I walk away, apologetically, not sure my satisfied curiosity was worth its trauma.

SANTA AMALIA

IT IS FRIDAY NIGHT I THINK, even if the days have now mostly collapsed, first under the rotation of wheels; of riding to sleeping to riding; second with the weight of the pandemic's restrictions as they break all of our social rhythms.

The village of Santa Amalia sits opposite the steel pipes and smoking tanks of petrochemicals being fractured, and beside a road that courses with constant traffic. It reminds me of roads in poor countries, in that the town is so entirely separate from the road, which obviously came here after it, because the two have no real connection or relation to one another. The road simply passes the village. A walkway of high steps crosses over it, painted green, so that villagers can walk to the countryside the other side of the road. The road is both everywhere and nowhere. I imagine the village, the villagers, how peacefully they must once have crossed into the campo.

The streets of the village are full of young people. They are younger teenagers and older teenagers; those who are virus-resistant, or least virus-wary, I suppose. The teenagers make up most of those out in the square, though a few masked adults are still found in a bar, where a hunting programme screens on a television; adults watch the screen as a dead deer head is lifted at its antler by a man in camouflage and a beard. A glass cabinet against the wall displays hunting knives for sale in this, what they call Deep Spain.

Perhaps, in its own way, the scene simply shows the world as it was before; young people out in the streets without a building of their own to be inside of, and no money to spend in communal buildings, so that they live their life outside instead.

As I go through the village, I see more people appearing, dressed in masks. It is noticeable that people seem more diligent to wear masks at night, as if we have taken the illicit idea we have of nighttime and lent that morality to a virus that cares nothing for it. For the same reason, play seems to have been adjudged higher risk than work, even where the risk – outdoors, in fresh air – is often less. The message is simply that we should not play, and we should work.

In the main square, the kids separate into their two age groups; young teenagers and old teenagers. The young are louder, run back and forth, they are mischief. Two boys light a fire in a paper cup, a girl then throws on some matches, other bits of rubbish. It sparks, it catches fire; the budget pyrotechnics of bored youth, where you must make your own excitement because naturally so little occurs, but to accept living without it is not an option. A boy playfully jumps over the young flame;

I think of Newroz, Iranian New Year, and its jumping over a bonfire, celebrated all through the Persian and Zoroastrian worlds; up into the mountains of the Kurdish regions, down in Tehran, and so too the Kurdish neighbourhoods of Istanbul. I think how timeless and universal is the idea of jumping over fire.

The flame subsides to charred ash and a stain of soot upon what was so recently the ornamental, polished stone step of the bank in the village square. I imagine an angry bank manager on Monday morning. In the charred step, I think of those men who come to Istanbul from distant villages, who arrive with nothing, and so buy a metal kettle and break up pieces of wood to light a fire directly on the pavement beside the Bosphorus. And they boil water on their fire, and they drop in tea leaves to make cups of tea they will sell to the fishermen and the passers-by, and hope to begin building a life from the profits. I always wondered what it must be like for those men, new to the city; to see a pavement and in it see only the ground; the same ground you have always known in your village, but to neither care nor perhaps more than that, realise, that in the city the ground is different, because even the ground beneath your feet has been constructed, has been built, and the earth that in your village sustained you has been hidden.

On the other side of the square are the older teenagers; a smaller group, quieter. They do not run around, a boy not-so-subtly gives a flirtatious kick to the back of the leg of a girl, who kicks back, and so perhaps likes him too. They stand and watch the square, all in masks, hands in pockets, like they are waiting for something to begin, for adulthood. Here they stand, practising adulthood; saying and doing little, learning how not to say much, not to give themselves away, for as adults it is safer to define by what we are not, than by what we are.

I roll towards that darkness on the edge of town. I roll out of the main square, pass a church; a rounded belfry; the whole thing plastered with a matt clay, like a terracotta jug, old-looking, a simple cross from two varnished timbers high above, silhouetted against the moon.

I hear the road, still coursing, just as I left it. I see it. Cars pass; trucks; a tanker.

I think I see the world here: the people in the village, ready to sleep, protected by its walls, its square, its church. And then the road; the economy, which knows no sleep and floods by outside, and where the village will one day have to send its young, at least a few of them, in offering to the gods of money.

A sacrifice of children, if the village is to survive.

GUADALUPE HILLS

YELLOW BIRCH AMONG THE GREEN; so bright, so pure and so strong. I see it and I think of our world, where conformity always seems safest until it is too late, and people are so afraid to stand outside of a group, to be different in the ideas they will express. Everyone wants to assert their uniqueness but on their own terms, and nobody wants to be asserted unique by anyone else. To be unique on our own terms is to be special. To be unique on the terms of others is to be different.

I think of the men outside the bar in Deep Spain, who laughed at me as one but were afraid of the moment they must make the individual decision of when to stop laughing.

For the most part I try not to, but here, perhaps strangely, with this yellow birch so shamelessly different, I think politics.

The political system we belong to stands often for murder, misery and impoverishment, but it is operated politely. To condemn murder, misery and impoverishment is often to isolate oneself from the system of politeness. This is a sign that we value the politeness of some above the lives of others.

I wonder how to make humans more like this birch; indifferent to the mass around it, proud of its colour, irrefutable in this yellow, the colour of the truth.

Through the mist, at the roadside where I ride, I look at this yellow birch; so solid and strong, dependable and unashamed, a yellow flame within the green.

And on another level, I know it is only the sap in the leaves, hardening cold for winter, but before they fall.

GORGES

IT WILL BE ONE OF THOSE DAYS of ecstasy. But as always, I do not know it yet.

Inside the church I walk, across the step of stone where many others stepped before me. That smoothed marble no different to Süleymaniye Mosque, Istanbul; Dome of the Rock, Palestine. Worship; past gathering, ghosts of congregations in a world no more to gather, at least for now. I often look inside a church or mosque; something draws me to them, as if they are an attempt at an idea that I seek, even if I know that these places are not, for me, the real thing – at least not yet. I see the old oak pews, which still seem to hold in them the forms of those who sat there and the ideas they came for. At the altar, a wooden globe, carved. Angels taking flight. A lectern awaits its priest.

I sit beside candles pushed into a basin of sand, with hot translucent wax occasionally running down into it, turning white as it hits the cool grains, rolls over itself and sets. In front of me are the hymn books, slotted away, and as I pick one out and leaf its pages and words in a foreign tongue, I remember the hymns I was made to sing at primary school, and how innately they repelled and confused me with lines of how bad I was, how bad we all were. More than anything, I think I took issue with someone talking that way about my mum and dad.

In the corner of the church is the vestibule of the confessional box, a murmuring of Spanish from it; I am reminded that here, God speaks Spanish. Shapes move behind the rows of many small crosses cut from the wooden side of the box, both concealing and not concealing the priest and sinner, each of them playing their timeless roles from the stage of another small town.

Again, I take my leave, but riding on I make my own confession, unburdening, like removing a pannier bag at the end of a long day's riding. I once described my bicycle as a prayer mat, where I sat and lowered my forehead to the handlebars and then the ground in search of meaning. Perhaps riding is itself a form of confession, of affirming yourself upon the earth, asking it to take you as you are, to forgive you your trespasses.

And what then of my other solace, of writing?

I ride, and I write. They are my existence, they became my being. I still do not know how I executed this plan. I did everything a writer would do. First of all, I wrote. Second of all, I completed works. Third of all, I sent those works out to others, believing they should be read.

And by the time I did all that well enough, and repeated and learned where I did not do it well enough, I had come to present sufficiently convincingly as a writer that others too were ready to be convinced I was a writer.

But I prefer not to look at it this way. The people to whom I sent my works, they were just gatekeepers to publishing; a castle, a citadel, the insides and purpose of which I already knew better than many of them did. Although, if I consider it a moment longer, this is not entirely true either. Perhaps I knew the citadel, its holy book, but I confess I had no idea about the state of the latrines.

The most important advice, in writing or in life? Know yourself. Do not attempt to learn always what to do or what to write, because you cannot always do so. Learn who you are, and then you will get better at knowing what to do.

In writing, I made my dream my truth by insisting it would be so. There is an old photo of me in dungarees, a dummy in my mouth and surrounded by the books that I loved even then. Another of me, sat at a typewriter with chocolate spread around my cheeks, the dummy still in my mouth, and the same dungarees. My mother joked that I looked like an editor, that the dummy was like my cigar, that I was practising.

This is a half truth; the other half is helpful too. I also dreamed once of becoming a cyclist; a professional, a real one. I dreamt it, dreamt it hard in the lanes of Leicestershire and then further afield, before realising it would never happen for me. The 20mph I could stretch as an average over the flats would never compete with a Tour de France 25mph average even over mountains. I calculated that, perhaps with the gains of riding in the peloton, and a better bike, I might gain an extra mile an hour for each, but it still left me 3mph an hour too slow on average. I worked it out, that this dream was not for me. And that's OK too. You have to learn which ones are worth chasing, because as with all things, the chase is part of the joy.

One thing it's hard to understand beforehand is that it is not easy to live the other side of a dream, in the space where a thing you suspected would never come true eventually does. I think this is where a lot of the world's cynicism comes from, because dreams cannot be accrued. And after they have been met, or if in not being met they break the heart of the dreamer, then without a depth of soul and the desire to help others – instead of ourselves – achieve dreams, it is easier to start accruing simpler things instead. You can accrue more capital than you need, you can accrue status, you can now accrue followers, although it is hard to say how far they would follow you. All things considered, these are bad dreams, and – however hard it is to muster, whatever damage they do – their dreamers warrant pity. People pursue these things because they have no real dreams.

It is a truth insufficiently spoken that our world now struggles most of all with a want of real dreams. Too much power rests with algorithms, and because algorithms have no need of sleep, they also produce no dreams.

As I ride and write my heart, I wonder, am I giving myself away? Is my writing a confession? To let you in on a secret, if you live fast enough you can write everything without ever being confessional. By the time your last words are being read you've already moved on to new ones; the past is another country, unrecognisable from the present. The words describe a different person, a stranger.

Besides, the objective is to live large enough, to feel deep enough, that yours is never an individual life anyway. You try to experience it all. You listen to others, compulsively, and so your writing becomes not you but a collage of universe. You try and write for everyone, a goal at once both ridiculously overblown and yet deadly serious. Of course sometimes you fail, but it is the only task worth trying, and, on some level, the duty of a writer.

After this, you must feel hard and think clearly. This is not always easy, because they are opposing traits, where feeling hard obscures a clarity of thought, and clarity of thought comes often at the expense of feeling.

On life's tightrope, you venture forth.

In others, too, you must keep your heart large. A writer should be like a lawyer for the human soul; nobody is beyond redemption, every failing and wrongdoing is to be met with explanation above blame; identifying a version of the world where it need not have been so, where the hurt can be cured. The writer must mark that path.

The bicycle and the book always reminded me of one another. The bicycle is powerless without its rider, just as the book is powerless without its reader. And yet, together, the bicycle makes its rider more than mortal, in the same way that a book lifts its reader upwards. Both of them take you, take you up to the high places, although sometimes, I resign myself to the fact that I will never write the road so perfect as it was to ride. And that, that is how it should be.

I'm sorry, but look at me. I've written the contents of my head across these last hours, and not mentioned the road at all, which for a while leant me its clarity of thought. Let me tell you.

In some ways, it all appears as one; now it is just a series of images, resplendent, that my eyes took in as my mind ascended to a reverie of wind and rain and cold, with lungs crashing and life, all life.

The grasses flooded golden, that much I remember clearly, and the road wound up and up, over more than seven hundred metres in the end, right into the cloud, where the silhouettes of trees leaned over the road and their dark forms were cut from the white mist like paper-chains in a classroom at Christmas with all the children laughing.

In and out of gorges I rode; they were gorges of granite, all grey and cold but somehow so warm, comforting in their permanence. A stream tumbled through rock and grass, and the foaming white of churned water spoke to me:

Wash your mind, write calm.

And round crooked bends I moved along roads that opened to wide valleys, where the greens of pines brushed against the reds of autumn, and small drifts, swirls of white cloud floated as if we were all together in some perfect painting where the road hugged close to the rock and asked for safe passage, carrying its rider over it.

At the top there was a radio mast, and below it was a sign for the land of La Mancha. I looked up at the mast in its series of red triangles and trusses, pointing straight up into the cloud tearing across it with its rain, and I looked at the mast with the drums of signal boosters and antennae sticking out at all angles so that we could communicate with one another. And I remember that those shapes and right angles in their red looked so perfect against the cloud. Then I took a photo, something I do from time to time at the head of a pass and with its nameplate. Me, smiling, hair slicked wet. Its name:

Puerto de San Vicente – 807m

Once over the rise of the peak, the wind hit me. Then I learned that the wind had been coming from the north, and the steep wall of the climb had without my knowing it been my shelter. The wind came hard and the wind came fast. It stung a temperature of winter against my bare legs, my knuckles, brought the calendar forwards and lashed new rain from out of the sky.

Oh but how I smiled, and how light I felt, as if there at last the restrictions of the city and the pandemic left me finally, if only for a moment, and my lungs and my heart, they beat as one in that place where all the emotions they meet as one. Chill to the bone but happy, I plummeted down the other side.

HOTEL MARIA JESUS

RAIN INTENSIFIES. I ride off the main street, loop a roundabout, ride a smaller road, looking up and down the adjoining lanes. There is nothing. A man buried deep in a raincoat, head down, walks from a house:

"Excuse?! Señor!" He looks round. "Dónde uno hotel, pensión?"

He shakes his head, stupid question style. He waves an arm. "Talavera de la Reina!"

I sigh, call out. "Combiano kilometre?"

"Viente!"

Through cold rain and wind, nevertheless, we persist. My feet are cold, the colours of euphoria are fading and I am developing concerns for what happens next. As we descend what should be exhilarating bends and slopes, beside the edge of new valleys and hills. I am coming to appreciate the value of those more expensive brake pads and wheel rims that help to displace surface water and improve braking. I am not coming to appreciate this in a good way; Miles has neither thing, and so every bend feels like the cusp of death − I cannot slow my speed because my brakes run out of brake; they are all noun, no verb. It is one of those times when the coming hill is a relief, an incline to warm your body again, and to give you control of your speed once more.

Tavalera comes: a long village just off the main highway; a large village, a small town. There is a post office, church, a village square, shops and cafés shut but unmistakably there. I look around; there is no hotel and all the streets are bare.

A woman is saying goodbye to a man, the engine of his pickup running outside the front door as she stands under the shelter of the porch. Rain falls off the top of it, her arms folded as a temporary protection against the cold before returning inside. She straightens at the stranger coming towards her.

"Señorita...una hotel?" I point at the ground. "En Talavera?"

She lightens at the respectable question, easy to answer and a pleasure to help.

"Sí! Sí," and she waves an arm down the street we're on. "Directo!"

A few more minutes pedalling and there it is; a vertical line of large green squares with yellow letters bolted to the side of the building:

I
I-H
I-O
I-T
I-E
I-L
I
I
I

And then the name: Villa Maria. And yet...and yet it looks closed.

There is a large doorway with flecked marble tiles, a dry place in which my subconscious has I think instantly decided we will stop and sleep the night if necessary. Everything looks closed, so closed it might never have been opened and will certainly never open again. A buzzer, with no words on the label beside it, that looks unpressed and unimpressed at the idea of being pressed, of being interrupted in its hundred year slumber. I press it. I press it hard and hold it down, for either someone must hear this – I will compel them to hear this – or else there is no owner around to hear it and so it's all the same to them and to me anyway.

I press. I wait. And nothing. I press and I wait…and nothing. I stand back, I look out at the road and the rain. I close my eyes, softly; the closed eyes of resignation meeting contemplation. Somewhere in heaven a soft piano key is also pressed, giving a high note. And then, on earth, a noise; just one noise, more mundane, and yet a decisive noise, from nowhere and out of the silence. It is only the sound of a button somewhere else having been pushed, releasing electricity, so that from the latch in front of me, a small but perfect sound;

click.

I push at it, and the door creaks; creaks perfect, creaks haunted. The lobby has not been stood in for a while; it is dim and shadowy. A front desk is there at the foot of a staircase. An old woman is standing at the top of the staircase; a little hunched, hair tied back, face looking out of its wrinkles and right at me like I must be mad, like she's mad, and who in all hell has she let in, but damn she needs the money.

"Sí?"

She asks, as if I am either God or a murderer and either way she must await my judgment.

"Hola! Habitación?"

"Sí," she replies, a little surprised, but like that's OK and, coincidentally, exactly what she does, her line of work. She shuffles down the steps, pulls me inside. Dismayed at the wet. Waving all of it in; the bike, the bag on the pannier rack. She is personally distressed at how wet I am.

"Habitación?" She says.

"Sí" I say.

"Solo?" She looks at me, holds up one finger.

"Sí."

She gives a nod, as if this is OK, as if this will be OK. I stand there and right away she pulls paperwork from a drawer, as if to get on with it before I can change my mind.

Beside us on the wall is a large and yellowed roadmap of Extremadura meeting La Mancha. The main roads run as red veins and everything else is traced in black. I look over the terrain I've covered. The lobby, like the rest of the hotel, has not been cleaned for some time. The map has not been dusted either, and a few kilometres south of the city of Cuenca a large spider has either curled and died upon the map, or is in fact a symbol indicating something real out there in the world. If so, the villagers of Olmeda del Rey, just beyond one of its long and reaching legs, are in trouble; big trouble.

The woman gives a cough to turn my attention back to her. She smiles, hesitant. She points up to the wall where there is a vent in old, hardened black plastic. She turns to a panel of buttons and flicks one, up and down and up again; a red light in and out with it, and warm air coming from the vent. She points up to my room to indicate the same system, takes my wet sweater and holds it up before the vent, to indicate what I should do; that this will create dryness.

She smiles, but this time with some enthusiasm, as if letting me know again and definitively that I'm going to be OK. She goes into a drawer beneath the counter, pulls out a key and slides it over to me; the key fob the same green-yellow as the sign out front. There is a name on the reverse of the fob to the key she hands me: Maria Jesus

I look at her, try to look kindly; for everything about her is timid, meek, and yes, is just that, is kind. I try to look like I'm saying hello, but saying it properly, asking her name.

"Maria Jesus?" I say, trying to intonate a question.

And wide-eyed she looks up at me, like it's the police asking.

"Sí?"

Maria Jesus, so humble she's barely even there, as if it wouldn't be right to take up the space. I put my hand to my own breast:

"Julian. Julio."

And I smile, and I nod as she does the same, and puts her hand to her own chest with a relieved sort of a smile back as she says her name, her sweet name:

"Maria Jesus."

LA MANCHA

MAINTENANCE

MILES IS IN WORSE SHAPE than I thought. He creaks and groans and one of his cranks constantly winds itself loose and I suspect will eventually break off. The gears rattle and sometimes squeal, and then drop a cog and send me falling fast as the chain slips. I could curse Miles to damnation, but don't quite because I know he could get worse, and that I might be punished for my negativity with further problems that make me miss and feel retrospectively grateful for what I had. Sometimes I enter a good mental space, and I treat all his squeals and shrieks as just experimental jazz from his namesake spirit; a really challenging album, like 'Bitches Brew' but harder stuff. It took me about a week to come up with this notion, and it was a healthy discovery, because it meant I was finding a peace with circumstances. Sometimes I can't hear Miles, I forget that he is there, and once the sound returns to my consciousness I cannot comprehend what heights of zen I must have achieved to block out that noise, that accursed noise.

There are however still the liberties that come with the fact Miles is such a bad bike. For starters, I can never go fast. It is futile to try and go faster, which is an impulse that ruined many a bike ride. Because Miles will never go fast. Miles' fastest remains slow. When the morning came, and I was slow in riding, there used to be this sense that with the passing road I would accelerate as my muscles warmed up. This is no longer a problem, because whatever happens to me, Miles will never warm up. Miles was born cool.

Best of all are the ascents, the long and slow inclines where I travel at such a crawl and fear I might snap the chain before the wheel turns into a new rotation. I have cycled 50mph on a Pacific tailwind across the Texas plains, and I have sped down from the mountains of Kazakhstan into the deserts and cities of Uyghur that should never have seen the suffering they since have. But let me tell you, you have not known freedom on a bike until you just get off and fucking push. And know that that's OK.

I get off, take Miles by the handlebars, and at a respectable pace and with far less effort, I push him up and over the rise, as if there's simply no hurry. Like there's no place to get to anytime soon.

For this life lesson, I have Miles to thank.

PATIENCE

WHENEVER THIS HAPPENS, I think about patience. The first thing that comes to mind when I consider patience will always be a moment in East Kazakhstan, as I pedalled towards Almaty, some 300 miles from the Chinese frontier. It was the Eurasian leg of my ride around the world and, all told, would have covered by its end all the land between Lisbon and Shanghai.

The roads in Kazakhstan are of an order long, straight and empty in a fashion unknown in Europe and that do not, going east, begin until at least the Ukraine. A road, unbroken by bend, will unfurl thirty straight miles to the horizon, and anything on it is clearly visible so long as the very curvature of the earth doesn't obscure it before that sight arrives.

For maybe three or four minutes of pedalling, a dark silhouette of black on sun-white landscape moved my way, the two of us sharing the same edge of the same side of the road. As it neared, the silhouette appeared as only legs and a torso, walking. Closer still and there emerged the brim of a sun hat, in a style unlike any Kazakh would wear. Closer again and, though the face and its features – like the Kazakhs – was East Asian, it looked different to those locals I had seen. Slowing to a halt in front of one another, the man appeared to be pulling behind him a trailer, the holding of which meant his arms disappeared out behind him, leaving only the outline of torso and the beginnings of shoulders.

We stopped in front of one another, greeted. He was Japanese, his trailer contained camping gear, spare tyres for the wheels that pulled it, camera equipment and a couple of gallons of water. He was skinny, standing in a vest, long shorts, sturdy boots, the hat with its wide brim.

Over the years, many have said in response to my journeys by bicycle that I must be very patient, but this compliment – if that's what it is – is one I have always struggled to respond to. It is an unusual compliment, not necessarily right for a mere 'thank you', but more than that, I struggled to respond because I always felt it untrue. Am I patient if, as I ride, I grit my teeth and imagine, fantasise, the enemies and adversaries of the world that my pedal strokes will vanquish? Am I patient if I do battle with and mull the challenges I will wage once I return home?

To me, the bicycle has always been a quite impatient vehicle, or at least a sink into which I could usefully pour out my own impatience. In pedal and in crank, the machine gives me power always to go faster, or else to try and go faster, to hurry. Over short distances, in cities, the bicycle is anyway faster than anything else. Over long distances, the bicycle and the vastness of the earth's terrain, combined, have made me more patient;

but they forced patience upon me. This equation of geography plus human power has disciplined me, perhaps, but I myself, I still regard as impatient. Without the bicycle, my mind flits, and so by its focus, the bicycle improves me.

Whatever my own feelings, this label has been given to me, and each time I was called 'patient' I would mumble some thanks while thinking the label only odd. Then, at a roadside in Kazakhstan, me and the Japanese man, walking with the trailer, crossed paths, and greeted one another.

"Are you walking?" I asked, though it was obvious.

"Yes," he nodded, "from Shanghai."

My eyes widened, "to where?"

"Lisbon."

He would walk every mile of that same 13,000 I would eventually have cycled. I must have half-laughed, and though I had always thought the remark silly, all that I could say, as maybe you have guessed, was:

"You must, you must be so patient."

The man looked awkward, perhaps as I always had when met with this compliment, and finally smiled, perhaps as I always had. He scuffed his shoe in the dust.

At the time I was heading for Urumçi, where I had heard of an escalating crackdown against the local Uyghur Muslim population, who had long resisted their repression by Chinese authorities. There had been protests and unrest and, knowing that I'd be there within the week, I had been concerned for what I would find.

"I'm going to Urumçi, next week. I heard there had been rioting. Was it safe there?"

"It was OK," he paused, "but I walked there three months ago."

We wished one another good journeys and went on our way, at our different paces, where I would arrive in days across a distance he had spanned in months.

It went beyond only that, however, and since then I realised patience was more than a question of only the absence or presence of haste. In the years that followed, the virtue of patience came to seem all the more precious, as the politics of the world seemed to falter into erratic accelerations.

It was clear, almost too obvious to mention, that if you did not like the way of the world, if you perceived injustice in it, then what you needed was change. That word 'change' in particular, was only par for the course in the speeches of any two-bit politician. But, if you are identifying a way in which the world is flawed, and the way you would like it to be better, the one thing that any movement will without doubt require, more than money or people or newspaper coverage, banners or political votes, is the ability to wait; is patience.

Does the bicycle teach patience? Maybe. Many years ago, the first time I rode alone to Istanbul, passing two hours, fully loaded with bags over the beautiful Col du Lautaret that holds France from Italy, I realised that to reach the summit took two hours going slow and two hours going fast. Perhaps there'd have been some difference, perhaps five minutes if I really pushed… but really, it was two hours.

Further into that journey, struggling without water on an unexpected mountain pass above Montenegro's Golf of Kotor, I laboured, glancing above and seeing only more crash barriers wrapped to so many turns still unclimbed ahead. I realised that looking up, fatally, had slowed me down and sapped at my will; to try and see the place of my future higher up the mountain had only burdened my present on the ascent. I just had to pedal, to be patient, and so wait for the outcome of eventually passing over the top.

Since then, the world went speeding up; patience becomes ever harder to come by, to preserve, too. Chronophobia, the fear of time, comes for us and events that felt like years ago are in fact, it transpires, from only February.

Did the internet make us all impatient? Did the stock market, with its promise of riches if only a chart would climb higher? Did the media, with its promise of insight at the end of the column's inch? Did opinion polls, with their promise of knowing?

In acquiring the tools to plan and span the entire world, perhaps we had lost both patience but also an accurate sense of time. Our circadian rhythms had broken, and we forgot the one and only thing that can slowly change the world: it takes a village.

In all that, I thought ever more about how the bicycle did, just maybe, help to restore my patience. My movements between places became journeys, not merely departures and arrivals, so that they lifted me momentarily out of time and became their own distinct events, threaded together and each with meaning.

But still, there was more to it. I remember once being asked by someone, possessed of the supreme wisdom of youth, which is in fact only courage by another form:

"Do you think patience is more important than it used to be?"

She went on, hers that sort of spirit determined to ask questions born of a burning need to understand and improve this world of ours; the sort of question age steadily forces from us, trammelled, as our minds and bodies tire and we get on simply with the business of dying.

I said that "yes", perhaps it was, perhaps she was right. Patience had become more important.

To which she responded:

"But don't you think patience is arrogant? That it assumes superiority, as if you will be proven right in the end, and all you must do is wait?"

Was patience in fact arrogant? That was a new thought. Surely waiting could not be arrogant, for patience was passive – or was it?

Patience agrees to vacate the stage awhile, to leave space for other ideas to exhaust themselves. Patience gives them enough rope. Patience assumes it will prevail, just like the bicycle over the mountain climb. Is that so wrong? Perhaps it means patience is active; for it watches, it must replenish itself and must wait in the face of stupidity or hypocrisies, injuries assembled like whole mountain ranges. Patience must endure.

The same force that compels it to vacate the stage makes patience a benevolent force; it declines to assert itself on another, and instead waits for its adversary to tire, to subside. Patience expects eventually to win because it is right, which is perhaps an arrogance, for what truly can be regarded 'right', in absolute terms? Very little, surely; not much more than a refusal to coerce, to allow the exploitation of the vulnerable – these are ideas in which one can believe absolutely, and without accusations of arrogance.

And so, patience perhaps is revealing to us, more significantly, something other than itself – a thing not at all passive and more profound than merely waiting.

Patience, followed to its logical conclusion, is really only a symptom of something else; it is a garment worn and used by that greater body we now and then, and in certain ideas, find ourselves able to possess:

Faith.

TOWARDS TOLEDO

WILL I FIND PURPOSE AS I RIDE? Should I have more purpose? Will I find it when I arrive? Arrive where? I ask myself all of it as I pedal.

A puddle at the roadside bursts with a frog landing into it, displacing the equivalent of its mass in water. I hear the droplets land with a patter, and it resembles the manufactured sound on a phone alert, though made by nature and physics, and unique. I consider how minimal and soothing the stimulation of the real world and its chance moments are compared to the bleeps, alerts, the push, the ups and downs and prompts that snag and snare my attention back home.

At times when riding, this is all I can imagine doing happily with a life right now. I almost fear, in some moments, the time when I will stop pedalling, which before long, when the land runs out, I know I will have to. The movement, superficial but literal, has been the closest I've known to a sense of change, or even the possibility of change, for six months. The pandemic is its own set of obstacles, and yet it somehow underlines how rigid and half-empty the world we were building was to begin with; a life in the shadow of what a life could be.

I ride the A-roads; national highways but not full motorway. I feel the country opening; roads spread further and straighter before my eyes, with space for them to occasionally flatten rather than only climb towards the next ridges of the land. I move naturally through perhaps a hundred kilometres a day, I take to highways, busier roads, I get that old itch, and try to increase my distances up towards one-two-five, and then one-fifty.

Fortunately, I always had a sort of fondness for highways. They are less scenic than the back routes, but they always helped with the thing about cycling that most enchanted me; the fact I could cross an entire country or continent.

I consider the different categories of road. The lanes, which perhaps reward the most patient – the historian, the scholar – show us the past; a world of waterwheels and orchards and stone walls and ruins. In lanes you can see the world as it was. At the other extreme is the motorway; where perhaps you see the future and the world as it will be. Placeless, humanless, identical; radar-controlled speed and radar-controlled tolls. What personality the motorway has is forced into it in contrived shops, service stations that simulate warmth or home or nourishment; squirty cream hot chocolates, bright toys, slogans and posters, an overstatement of life to make up for the absence of life.

My choice has often been the A-road, the highway; the middle of the two. Though sometimes too busy, they became a little like my laboratory; my research post. They show the suburbs with their outsized control over our politics. They show the family business which is always struggling, the interaction of industry and poverty and extreme normality which is where most people live. They show the out-of-the-way places where people of lower economic or lower social value are put. Here, the land moves between grain silos, the polytunnels of industrial plum tomato farming, the acrid stench of nightshade from the tomato canning factory. And then the ruins of Roman amphitheatres and suggested tourist detours that point to them.

MEDIAN

TOLEDO, I REALISE, is to be a halfway point. It is a halfway point firstly because I realise Miles will not make it much beyond Barcelona, if that. At the same time, I hope he can get that far, because Barcelona and the Mediterranean would seem a nice ending, a place of poetry, a fine bit of final punctuation. Toledo, however, is also a halfway point because, down to a few dozen miles, it must be as near to central as it gets in the Iberian peninsular; a median point, a natural half, a heart to my journey. Mi Corazón.

This halfway point, however, after I have decided on it, brings with it other consequences I had not foreseen. Firstly, if there is a half then by definition there must be a whole. And if there is a whole then all this has limits and has an ending. When I set off from the Atlantic, moving east and only that, the process was undefined and so limitless. The process was all there was. It was a sphere; one of wheels, globe and sun, all three orbiting, and so, limitless. In this halfway point, even one so fair as Toledo, my ride and its existence has been met with accountancy. I have done one of those few things that define humanity and separate us from all other forms of life. I have formed a plan, I am envisaging a future, and depending on whether I can move naturally and healthily towards it, this future has the opportunity to advance or to curse me – to move me forward, or suffocate my ability to exist without the spectre of the future.

The last problem of a half way point is that there is now, for one final moment, as much ahead as behind, and thereafter, more behind than ahead. My past, as pasts tend to, will grow bigger than my future, and I will be tasked with finding happiness in my ability to be content with my past, and hopeful for my future. Such is the basic trial of life. Was I happy? Can I be happy again? And therefore, most crucial of all; am I happy?

REGRET

THIS WAS NOT MY FIRST TIME HERE. Toledo came into my story once before, on a late November night ten years ago. I was about one week from the end of a circumnavigation around the world; 18,000 miles in which I broke a world record set by a man who had ridden in conjunction with large banks and corporate investment funds. As I saw it, he had broken not only a world record on that ride, but also the spirit of the bicycle, and the spirit of adventure. Worst and more unforgivable still, and despite the fanfare and bluster, he had been slow. His record had been 193 days and looked miserable. Mine was 169. And I had so much fun.

But not that night at Toledo. I remember I looked down on the city and how perfect it had appeared; a perfection that from inside its walls I now realise was true, every bit of it true. The night was cold, the sky ink blue and glowing with the lights of the Alcázar and with the lights of the cathedral. And though it looked so pretty, I had another thousand miles to ride in perhaps just seven more days, and the descent of that hill into the bowl of the city beside the River Tejo, which last I crossed outside Lisbon but flows here in Toledo too, was too much to consider.

And so, I rode on into the night, up through the hills and through the olive groves and mountains, that come the dawn would break and show me Madrid. But as I looked down at Toledo that night a decade ago, and as I rode out of it, I think a small part of me promised myself that I would come back.

I don't like the idea of revenge and I don't like the idea of regrets, but perhaps, in Toledo, I can live with the idea that by being here again, I can take revenge on a regret, gently.

TOLEDO

PRESSED INTO THE RED brick walls around me are small white ceramic tiles, some with blue Magen David, and others with words of Hebrew. I am seated at a café inside the old Jewish Quarter of Toledo, from which the forebears of a friend from Jerusalem were expelled five centuries ago, and so that his family became Palestinian Jews, along with so many thousands of Muslims and Jews from Spain.

At my table a small plate of cured meats has been placed, and I consider the intersection of this history and this food. The unrivalled range of Iberia's pork charcuterie originates from the efforts of those Muslims and Jews the medieval Spanish state was intent on converting to Christianity. People innovated and experimented to disguise the flavour or texture of pork, or suggest its presence where there was none, ready for the visit of Christian authorities who would demand to see them eat it as proof of a genuine conversion. Our cultures always travel perhaps strongest of all in our food, which it is strange to think in this pork, created something so pleasant out of a necessity so sinister.

Next door an old lady steps out of her restaurant with a parcel of kitchen roll. She crouches down towards a small cat, unwraps the perforated paper to reveal a mashed ball of poultry scraps. She smiles, smiles an old wrinkled face that breaks to a dozen other smaller smiles. Smiles on her cheeks, her forehead, smiles around her eyes. The cat purrs.

In front of me the waiter laughs, wide-eyed and happy as he tilts the bottom of the bottle of red in front of me, inviting another glass. I laugh too, for his face is one of pure joy, and just as it is the job of a good tailor to make you feel beautiful in his clothes, to let you know that you look good in them, so too will a good waiter let you know you look good drinking his wine. That with a glass in hand, the world will smile at you, with you.

And so, I gesture another, and he smiles. And he pours.

REPAIR

IN THE QUIET OF THE OPEN ROAD, a small whistling tune is coming for me. The sun is still bright, warm, the afternoon young, I am carefree. But I think I see a softness appearing in the front tyre. I push at the handlebars; force them downward into the fork, into the axle, into the wheel, and the tyre finally splays into its own softness.

I stop. I look. The white club-head of a thorn sticks from the rubber. I leave it in place, for I suspect it is still slowing some of the air in finding its way out, barring the exit. Miles and I are at a roundabout, which I race to as fast as Miles will race, wanting this last, precious air in the lung of my tyre to carry me as far as it can. The roundabout has a signpost, and the turning I had planned shows 8km to the next town. The turning I didn't want shows just 3km. And so, we must have a change of plan.

I pedal, I roll as fast as Miles will go. I hit a steep hill and begin to drop down it but now the sides of the tyre are being pulled flat against the tarmac and there is a danger of the metal rim skidding loose into any crack or none. And so I must push.

Here we are. It has happened. I have a puncture repair kit, though I did not buy a pump, reasoning that I could walk to where I could get a pump easily enough. And now that is exactly what I must do. My hypothesis will be tested.

As I push, I ask myself the questions: will I find a bike shop, will I find a garage? Will I – most embarrassing of all – be forced to knock a random door in this country all shut-up, and ask in English, or in all likelihood in mime, for a bicycle pump? I look at the bike, keeping all worry out of my mind, for it will only sap the energy I need in the coming hours of getting this fixed. In almost all circumstances, worrying is waste. Do not worry, plan, though do not chide yourself if a little anxiety enters your planning, for kept on a short enough leash, anxiety will show you eventualities you could never have foreseen, and can even be a friend of sorts.

I was half prepared for this puncture, but half unprepared. I suppose I was willing to wager that it might not happen. There was a puncture, and so I lost my bet. Or rather, for now, I have lost half of my bet.

The 3km to the village closes; I see its spread of houses, some warehouses at its edge. The road up the hill leads into the heart of its built area, which looks a good size, like it might work out, though I do not want to raise my hopes. The final kilometre begins, and at the top of the hill, where the road bends in towards the village centre, it is already just as I planned it. My decision not to worry is vindicated, for this Spanish town is exactly as I would have designed. I see the black-orange-red, and the waved word, Repsol, on a crest against the sky. The sign below shows no prices for the gasoline, but all I need is air.

Until now, my approach to Miles and his riding has been that of the Buddhist monks who will not work, but as a matter of conviction rely instead on fate and the donations of strangers, who support the monks because they in turn appreciate the opportunity to be giving, generous. My approach is that of the particularly pious Salafi Muslim men who have a certain mustiness of smell to them, because they will wash hands, head and feet five times a day at prayer, ablutions as instructed by the Quran, but see any more than that as going against instruction. I am the Orthodox Jews who disavow the state of Israel in its entirety because to seize the land of Palestine was to interfere in God's work. My approach to Miles and his roadworthiness has been this same light-touch; a strict non-intervention.

At the current moment, however, at this roadside of Spain, my ideology with Miles must change, must adapt. Purposeful non-intervention is over. No longer can I maintain that the road and events must take their course and will determine the answers, or at least answers I will respond to only where I have to. Fate has indeed taken its course, and now I must offer some resistance to fate. We can learn to be reactive in life, but at some point we must be proactive. I must repair the puncture.

Looking down at the wheel, I see also the nut on the end of the axle, and in my quest for a pump, I realise I have forgotten that I will also need a spanner. Pulling on my mask, I walk towards an attendant; dressed in jeans and a shirt and freshly shaved this morning. I like this garage, it is as garages used to be I think; where a human being owns it, and repairs are done here and people earn a real living. Nobody is wearing the polo shirt of the large oil company that owns the premises and pays them minimum wage to sit here, repairing nothing, and only selling petrol and chocolate bars.

I can see the air line on the forecourt. I "Hola señor" and gesture down to the wheel, gripping an imaginary spanner and undoing a nut from its bolt in mid-air. The man gives a wave of his arm, off to one side and a hangar with an open door, shouts loud:

"Tony! Una llave para el hombre!"

I give a gracias, I walk over to the hangar. Outside the wide open doors that reveal nobody, I call a muted "Señor?!" Which seems impersonal and gets no response anyway, and so I too call out louder into the darkness: "Tony?!" Which I have learned to be his name, but seems too personal so soon.

Again I call into the dark hangar: "Tony, Tony?"

And I don't see him, but then a voice calls "Hola!" and I look up to see Tony, standing atop the ladder that leads up to the top of a tanker, hauling hoses into position. "Hola!" I call back, then gesture to the wall, where spanners and pliers and hammers and files are all in place on a board, their outlines drawn behind them. "Sí! Sí! Claro, claro!" Tony calls down, waving towards it with both hands as if I should be using his tools already, as if asking were almost rude rather than polite, as if he might ever have said no.

I undo the wheel, the tyre now so slack on the rim that I can pull it right off. I take out the tube. There is the rubber smell. There is the fish scale smell. There is Bina Clinica and all the other shops. But more than that, as I find the hole beneath the thorn head, as I apply glue and watch it immediately turn tacky in this strong, dry wind. More than that and there – pressing down hard on the patch with my thumbs – are the lessons from my grandfather in this very procedure, as a child, sitting on the kerb outside his house and also pressing a patch to a rubber tube.

He came from a generation of building and riding go-karts, motorbikes; of making the furniture for his house; of being drafted into the war effort and manufacturing the wooden propellors of spitfires during World War II. He made everything himself. From rhubarb to runner beans, he grew everything himself. And he fixed everything himself. Before I was even ten he had taught me how to fix a puncture, so that, like learning a language as a child, I now do it naturally. I consider my grandfather paying £5 for a new inner tube, rather than a lesser amount to be able to repair a puncture an almost infinite number of times. I think of my grandfather paying a further £10 to have someone else replace the tube in its wheel for him. He would have been holding the side of his forehead in his hand and standing with a confused smile if I told him such things now happen most of the time. I know his opening words on learning this: "By Jove."

I often considered, when repairing a bicycle, how the modern world steals our time so that we cannot ourselves do the things that we like, the things that restore us; the bike repairs, the gardening, the cooking, the playing with our children. Instead, the world gives us money, so that we can pay others to do these things for us, while we do jobs we perhaps dislike. Often those people who do our jobs for us – the mechanics, gardeners, bakers, minders and chefs – are left to do the job we like so intensively and repetitively, that the joy is soon lost also for them. I suppose that this is just capitalism, or at least, what economists call 'comparative advantage', where each of us specialise in just one thing. To whom this advantage falls, I do not know. Perhaps the advantage is to the Market, which turns this advantage into capital, and in the monetary profit, is our mutual loss of joy.

In front of me, looking down, the patch is fusing with the tube of the tyre. An orange orbit, a corona, flattens around the black patch, vulcanising, and I can almost see the two materials become one. There is a satisfaction here, because a minute ago this tube did not work, but now it will work again. This thing was broken and now it is fixed. It was bad and now it is made good. And on an infinitesimal level that somehow my soul will not ignore even if my mind can laugh at it; if this is possible in this one narrow element of life, then it must be possible also for all the world. Why wouldn't it be?

FLAGS

AFTER MY THOUGHTS about the end of Portugal's empire, Spanish street names strike me all the more. Cortés. Pizarro. There must be others that are names of Conquistadors I do not know. Standing beside a Cal Cortés, I think of Luis, who loves almost everything in this world apart from Spanish tourists in Peru, who he says walk around as if they own the place, and act as if they are returning home. I wonder if Portugal will have saved itself a headache here too; if, in already giving something so simple and small as an apology, it will be spared the total repudiation of empire that still awaits Spain, Britain, the United States or France, the last of which has yet even to realise its empire is gone.

As the days and the kilometres go by, and as the population grows denser than the one within the desert and scrub, I pass ever more people wearing masks. There are also, I notice, ever more Spanish flags embroidered on the masks. Perhaps in fear of the virus, the nation is the last hope of a saviour. I think of that post-Franco nation-building motto, those words: 'Spain indivisible', 'indissoluble'…lest the Basque or the Catalan or Galician get any ideas. Nowhere outside of the US do I think I have ever seen such prominence given to a flag.

Old men are perhaps, and perhaps not surprisingly, the greatest of all the devotees to the Spanish mask. They sit in chairs with aging legs so shrunken as to no more reach the floor. Or they stand, leaning and tapping at a cane, dressed in green corduroys and the Spanish flag over the mouth like duct tape on a kidnapped hostage, like an apple in a suckling pig; the perfect illustration of how nationalism and patriotism, whichever you prefer to call it, obstructs speech. Aging, with their flags over their faces, they are such perfect pictures of nostalgia, that thing where everyone eventually comes to think the past was better, but only because they were younger in it.

Sometimes, more gently, I look at them with their Spanish flags on their beaks, and against their withered skin, and as they move so weak and slow, I see the flags more innocently, perhaps for all that they are, stripped-back: I was here, this is where I stood, this is where I spent most of my time. This was home.

JAZZ DEALER

THIS ONE IS A SPECIAL PLACE. One hundred kilometres north of Albacete, Los Llanos: the planes. Where the scrubland and its long yellow desert grasses flood against the chain link fence of a small compound, where inside more grass and brush grows and tumbleweed rolls around a half dozen old cars, parked irregularly under the rusting shelter of a corrugated iron car porch.

One building sits in a corner of this abandoned-looking compound, and painted across it, wild and unruly as the grasses, is a phone number and a business proposition seeking second-hand cars for this, I guess, car dealership. In the corner of the building, however, with everything so rundown and ramshackle and in all ways unrefined, is an open window, and from it, falling out into the roadside, are the piano notes and rhythms of the most exquisite jazz.

I listen a while, and I think that this, here, is the world; in which I always find some new hope, if only because it demonstrates an infinite capacity to break expectations. In that power, this natural force of the world is able to collapse stereotypes with ease, by presenting me with a vision that is unique and before it is seen, one that I would never have guessed at.

Here is the precious truth that in all things, and in all individuals, is a greater power to defy a category than to conform to it, to bend a rule rather than confirm a pattern or preconception. For all its patterns, and by a vast majority the world is one of mostly unknown unknowns.

And in this power lies the even greater power, simply, for things to be different. To be changed.

DON QUIXOTE COUNTRY

PAST TOLEDO SOMETHING SHIFTS. The futility of Don Quixote's fable comes for me. How to act with chivalry? How to exist in a world when it hurts to? How to have values when the world does not? A truth: the hardest part of addressing politics when writing is to maintain your sense of dignity when so little that you see is dignified. The hardest part of political writing is to write that dignity with the keen clarity it deserves, while all around say that you're a fool for believing it at all.

More government warnings have been made. The towns are empty, everyone seems to be walking back to their houses, although even this is done awkwardly as this act is to admit they have been somewhere. People squeeze a little extra pace to get home before sundown. Children in masks ride bicycles across both sides of the road, like the town and its streets are finally theirs. Beside a river, floodlit, an industrial alcohol factory motors on, with pungent smoke pressing out of chimneys to fill the night, and a tanker loading cargo in a bay.

In the town centre a stone church and empty benches are cordoned off. Overlooking it is a mural: Don Quixote, looking down over his horse, with a large red heart, pierced by a lance. Never allow the separation of body from mind, never allow the separation of brain from heart. Bad politics often wins out because it is not ashamed to proclaim and practise the worst of all instincts, while good politics cannot, without blushing, speak the simple truth that the world need not be so.

In each town and even small village, at least one bar is still open and full of men with masks under their chin as if pants round their ankles in a brothel. Inside there is sawdust across the floor, tables with pots of rabbit stew upon them, where the men eating have forgone even the pretence of a mask; as if the stew is either a public health device, or is simply worth it. You see the men shout and laugh as they order more drinks across the bar. Each of them – for they are neither young nor healthy – may well in this proximity die of the virus, but the regularity, the irrepressibility, of these bustling establishments reads like a nationwide confession that Spain would die sooner, and indeed would sooner die, were this bar not open. This bar, the last place on earth where they can feel listened to, a hero in their own eyes, and maybe someone else's, once in a while.

TRAILS

FINALLY, I TAKE LEAVE OF THE ROAD; on to trails of white gravel that wind between fields ploughed brown and under a sky matt blue. Just once or twice a car or a farmer's van approaches; a tail of dust behind it and visible well in advance of the vehicle. I go between harvested vines, and the towers and steeples of churches mark the towns that I head for, weaving my way between the stone ruins of old farm buildings and hamlets no longer there. Signs mark the camino to Compostela, and I think back to my hiker in Portugal, a reminder that the camino is said always to start from your own door.

Up ahead, trapped but strangely so, a dog makes its way. The thing looks stray, put-out, and perhaps partly blind and deaf, for it will not leave the road, and nor does it look back at the noisy crunch of gravel and my chain. The creature pads beside a small pine plantation at the side of the track, where a large guard dog runs and jolts a chain fence with a bark, startling the stray, and for a moment I see it with its large ears shining like two pink lanterns in the sun. So as not to scare the dog, enjoying deep inside my soul the peace and the view of rolling hills, and with no interest to hear it bark, I get off and push Miles, so as to let the dog pull ahead. I see my shadow in the dusty trail; a new one to me, for normally I am atop the bicycle but here now beside it, arms across me. I smile at the newness, again, like I could get used to this; just pushing my bicycle.

On a telegraph line sit two pigeons, the same soft brown rust colour of the fields. They take flight as I near, alerting also a hare, its long ears full with sunlight as it bounds down the scrub, earth spraying from under it as the hare slides into a warren. Here, too, is garlic country; field after field, and then warehouses stacked high with crates of the stuff, so that all the air smells of aioli, bruschetta. A bulb with brittle purple-veined skin was dropped from a trailer to bake on the hot road; a few of its cloves turn golden with the oil seeping through, in need only of a wheel of camembert, perhaps a sprig of rosemary to make a feast.

On the edge of a town, I see a woman climb up to a stone wall. There are a line of olive trees over her shoulder, and she sits down cross-legged. She is young, in gym wear and headphones; looks to be doing a breathing exercise, perhaps a meditation. She turns into position, synchronised with my riding by, so that her back is always perfectly to me, and I cycle by forever unseen, never known to her in my strange sight. But I hope that she finds her peace, or that it finds her.

Farmers have lit fires in the verges between road and field. The verge is made up of a wild growth of dry thorn and thicket, all of which flames in an instant but, trapped between ploughed earth on one side and dry gravel on the other, has no fuel outside of itself on which to engorge and lose control. The farmer has yoked fire itself, an ox that now with flame ploughs clear this strip of land. I watch the fire move through the verge, through thistle, thicket, brush, crackling hot and lightning-quick beside me. Quick tongues of flame dance an orange that kisses everything black and then goes up in a clean smoke. This fire, moving through its fuel trapped before it, burns on until it exhausts itself, a force somehow reminding me of this virus, and on which we can only wait.

Arriving into town, outside a restaurant, I watch a waiter with a bottle of detergent as he wipes down each individual menu. It is strange to consider that such a routine act perhaps indicates our innate love for one another, our wish that people should continue with their lives, no matter how glittering or tedious.

I roll from the restaurant around to a garage. The last oil of Miles' chain is long gone and the chain howls all the more as a result. An old mechanic, a bit fat, dressed in comb-over and spectacles comes to me, hesitant at a stranger un-bid. His eyes follow my finger to where it points at the dry chain: "aceite?" I try. Then "huile?" He nods, returns with a long-nosed red oil can, the sort that belongs in my mind to the twentieth century, and he presses its little pump like a trombone key.

He stoops to my bicycle, a few presses build the pressure and then the drips come falling out the spout as opposite him I turn the pedal backwards, and the chain begins to run smoother under the drops of his oil can. Up and down the cogs he goes, making sure there is oil on each and every tooth, between each rivet of the chain. It is as if he knows that each drop is needed and will help me.

This oil is dark green-black. It is old oil, is wet oil, hardy; none of the aerosol stuff that will spray on in a silent mist and be washed away in the next shower. This is oil that will grip, will run to Barcelona. He smiles at me, happy as he finishes this job well done. As a courtesy, I ask if he'd like a little money for his troubles. He waves his hands across himself, his face looks hurt that I asked.

NIGHT — INIESTA, CUENCA

THE SUN IS GONE, my vision is only a black land under a black sky with a bright red line between the two and a red dot, the heart; the nucleus of an exploding atom, glowing bright where the sun disappeared fifteen minutes ago.

When I live indoors, I struggle most of all with not seeing the sunset every day. Each time it is like I am missing something special, a nightly miracle. Like there's something there on this earth that I should be more grateful for, and am taking for granted simply by not witnessing it. Every day indoors it happens like this, at dusk, this feeling of remorse.

I ride deeper into the darkness. From the loading bay of a depot, men call out instructions as a rig backs on to a dock. In five minutes of riding, the warehouse comes to an end. The horizon flashes, invisible and then not: night to red, night to red; a hum of electricity from the wind turbines, where the warning lights shimmer as the turning rotors pass shadows between me and them.

The firmament: Orion's belt is ever-present, straight and true, always more noticeable than Orion himself. I remember the name and location of few constellations, and none of the stories behind them, but I do remember at least a half dozen passwords, each with a number, special character, at least one upper-case letter, and associated memorable questions devised to trick fraudsters, though sometimes they also trick me, hinting at the worrying question that we should maybe in modern life ask ourselves more often: am I a fraud?

These passwords are the tasks to which our memories have been assigned, instead of the names of stars, trees, plants.

And there is only so hard you can fight the time into which you are born.

For a moment, I stop to rest. I walk around, stretching my legs beside my parked bicycle. I feel the cold on my body and give a quick shudder, uncomfortable, but I know that two weeks hence I'll be living in an apartment building again, and I know that I'll walk up to the highest hill above the city to watch the sun go down. And though it might be discomfiting now, in two weeks, that cold night wind across my cheek will be all that I want, and then, with a room to return to, I will remember it as being all the more delicious, all the sweeter, when that wind was also in my room for the night.

All night, Mars shadows the moon across the sky. In the last miles of this day's cycling, in the small hours, I see the beginnings of a shooting star. I see that quick trail of orange, and my mind prepares for the familiar sight that I love so. But no, this one is different; it is more than a shooting star and it is closer. Streaking downwards to earth, the orange catches spark, then flame, and bursts into tails of pinks and blues; a quick scar of colour on the night, as an asteroid burns up and falls to earth.

And as I see that collapsing meteor so pretty, from where I ride, I call out loud in delight. And yet, suddenly, at the same time, in its wonder, I am hit with a thought that might seem strange. As I watch those falling sparks on the night, I realise anew that the world cannot be improved only through exposure to its beauty, for in each day is enough beauty to melt a thousand hearts, and so I must resolve that people have grown inured to beauty alone, and we must have the need for change explained, and the faculty of shame rebuilt.

LONELINESS

As I RIDE THE NIGHT I consider if I am lonely, like a heartbeat, trying to find the stillness all-around of me. Sometimes I like to think of my heartbeat as one atrium answering the other. The buh always has, so far, its bhum. Buh-bhum. Buh-bhum. Sometimes, I extend the dialogue to include my lungs, whispering back. Sometimes I ride the night, alone, and I am my heartbeat, and I wait on the world to beat back.

I ride all night; thinking, always thinking. To think is easy and to act is difficult. Where I think, all the world can be made simple before me, and all my plans rolled out in an instant and without my having to lift a finger. To act out such a vision would take a millennium. But thinking, it is already done.

Some people think so much that they can no longer see the reality of what they witness. Or, they think so much that they are able to twist what they have witnessed into new and artificial forms that match their thoughts. Some people think so much that they will never act. I like to think as I cycle, because the body is as important as the mind. A thought is a thought but cycling is an act, and so, taken together, I'm reminded never to think in isolation of action.

The only thing worse and more dangerous than not thinking at all, is easy thought. Unfortunately, the acquisition of knowledge makes an intelligent person aware of their own ignorance, whereas one with less knowledge is also less likely to understand their own ignorance. This makes them confident, and people are less inclined to follow those who do not profess to have answers. Humans prefer to follow wrong answers than none at all. Perhaps, however regrettable, there is a certain safety even to this tendency.

Like a drug, these types of 'easy' thought make the world easier to cope with, they make it simpler. We take a group of people who have the same skin colour and we call them an ethnic group. We take a country that now and then holds votes in which most do not vote, we call it a democracy. It is easier to pretend that these names mean exactly what they are supposed to mean, than to address the ways in which they do not. We do not consider ordering people according to their favourite books, even though to do so might offer its own insight. These types of thought are a stimulant, or at least, they are an aid, a crutch for the brain. These types of thoughts are called abstractions.

The world is wholemeal bread, with a thick slice of cheese and petal of raw onion eaten with it, perhaps beside a roadside fruit tree with fresh windfall. With this thought I can ride all night. Abstractions are like pastries; refined sugar, delicious, an instant influx of energy, but an hour later I am on empty, and my head is tired.

The problem, however, is that just like a drug your threshold for abstractions increases, and so you need this kind of thought in ever greater quantities. The greater the quantity of abstractions you take, the harder it becomes to function usefully in the real world.

Opposite to abstraction, connection. The connection of humans was once essential to the physical functioning of human society, before industry, automation, and electricity made humans superfluous. Once, when human chains were necessary to the functioning of the life of the earth, everyone saw someone, once in a while; when felling the tree, when dropping off the bundle of firewood, when sweeping the chimney. Industry left us alone, so that we no longer came into regular contact with one another, and when we did, it would not be for long. Human connection remains emotionally essential, but not physically essential, and emotional needs are harder to see and to prove.

In the absence of other humans we have taken on ever more abstractions. When we do meet others, they are held right away to the expectation we have created in our minds of what another person is; a standard idea of how other people should be. And so, even where the person is able to disprove that standard form, still the bond of kin has been broken. Decency is reduced to a pleasant surprise, and when the person we meet errs from decency, it upholds the ideology that says other people are not like us, that other people are bad. Perhaps what is important here, more still than the bad or good which all of us at times exhibit, is simply that the people are Other, they are not of us.

To fill this void, media proliferated, and we fell victim to the tendency not to see other people, but the idea of other people. Where once the media was only the stories we told one another and built-up slowly, news now scrolls twenty-four hours a day, and lifelike depictions of fiction enter our brains with their own competing projections, one after the next. Our brains are not good at separating facts from fictions, they see only images of events, and recalls best that which went in deepest.

We know ever fewer people in real form, and ever more in the abstract form. This is a problem, because we find ourselves in our exceptions. Our deviations reveal us more accurately than our conformities, because in them we see what we hold sacred.

The absence of real people runs parallel to the absence of real places.

In this absence of real people and places, in the absence of the car dealership in the wasteland, run by a man who likes jazz and plays it loud, instead, we take up counterfeits.

Places are designed, places are standardised, places are surveilled and policed. These are counterfeit places, they are not real and were not made by us. We cannot be at peace in these places, and they cannot speak to the part of us that seeks individuality. And so, in the absence of our own individualism, we lose our sense of certainty.

If we cannot take certainty in a place, then we must create new certainty. Instead of certainty in place and people, we are provided with certainty in ideology. With ideology, which says that everything is fixed, a person has the power to reorder the world in a fashion convenient and recognisable to them. The scientist does not speak, the research is not real, the expert is not expert, and the mass-shooting did not take place, nor the war crimes of the war.

In Albacete, the jazz in the car dealership can be switched off, or never heard, or simply excluded from the calculation. Even though this jazz was all there was, and was all that mattered, it is easier to believe that no person in such a place enjoys listening to jazz. And so, deviations can be removed and counterfeits put in their place. Standing outside the car dealership in Albacete a person might well hear the music, but when imagining it from afar, they cannot. Given that few are likely to stand there, this is a problem; an information gap. The city sees the country in a view of its own choosing; the country looks back likewise.

In the early hours, as the towns begin to wake, I watch the people with me on the road. The street sweep. The delivery man. The pensioner. Another delivery man. A shop attendant unlocks a shutter, it crashes upwards.

When I ride, I rarely feel alone, because there are others all around, and more than that, I am open to those others. I believe in them and I believe in their goodness. I may be alone, but riding, it is more like being alone with the world. When you have faith in the world it is impossible to be alone. When you have lost faith then you have become a cynic, and the only solace you will find is in the company of other cynics; a company that only enhances your next loneliness.

In past journeys, as I travelled alone through the middle of the United States in all its emptiness, with its environment bleached of social interaction by mall and motorcar, I often thought that a part of its poor public information, its susceptibility to extremism, is down to its geography. In many parts of the country, you can travel a great distance under any order of misapprehension, and it will be a long time before you meet someone who is able to tell you, or remind you gently, by only their own alternative view, that you are an idiot.

Because you do not find your own truth alone. Solitude can help, but at root we are social beings. You find your own truth in company, or rather, in that word's fullest form; companionship. You find your truth by understanding the limits at which it offends others, or contravenes the interests of others, the truths of others.

Travel enough, paying attention as you go, and it will disprove every truth you hold at least once. In the end you are left believing in nothing but the immutable goodness of humans, all humans, and of their right to a just world.

The people I will see next morning – in the bar, in the shop – I believe that they are good. I care for them, and so I am part of a community. In many ways, the presence of the virus makes this community all the more obvious because, at its most elemental level, we would all like to survive it, and we would probably like everyone else to survive it, too, so that we are now closer than ever. Seldom do we go into an interaction so assured of having such a significant instinct in common as we do this summer. Even when you are alone, to belong to a community somewhere can be a greater companionship than a crowd or a conversation. Sometimes there is no peace quite like solitude, and no loneliness like the one you sometimes find in a room full of people.

For all that I feel that those cyclists I met at the roadsides are my lieutenants in humanity, there was one who later fell to loneliness. Artur. He spent too long out there alone, and in the end, it got him; a loneliness that runs deep enough to exclude the possibility of deviations. We met on the edge of Kazakhstan, close to China. Artur had just been driven out of Tibet by the Chinese police, having ridden in – all futile credit to him – with a Free Tibet sign across his handlebars.

We met together with Clement and Jean, who were riding from Lille to Delhi, as I pedalled to Shanghai. Artur had taken-up with them for a few days. To this day, I remain good friends with Clement, and for a while I asked also of Artur, who had finally, years after we completed our trips, cycled back towards Europe. Jean had moved to south Spain, and Artur had visited, in the end spending months on his sofa before one day setting off again. Finally, he had returned to Jean in Spain. Clement said sadly to me once,

"Jean says Artur, he changed. Like he was confused sort of. Like he had this idea of the world being one way, and like everything was already planned, and in the end, he wouldn't listen to anything else. I think maybe he spent too long alone."

PORTRAITS

LIFTING MYSELF UP out of my sleeping bag, I pull my hand through hair that is growing longer at my fringe, as if it is the rope that pulls the curtain up and wakes me. This morning an old couple stand over me; he in a wax jacket, she in a long coat and umbrella. We are just out of the centre of the village and the patch of grass, on a slope and beneath a tree, is just larger than my imprint on it. They speak, inquisitive rather than condemning, and he with a wave of the hand at my bedroom. A few sentences come out but no Spanish is necessary here, even with the "porque?" that forms a spoken question mark for me. In body language and expression, it is writ clear: 'Why are you sleeping here?'

I stop pulling at my hair, I look sheepish and think of the word for 'wild', to place before the word 'dogs' that in the night, with their barking so loud and close, had me move from the edge of this town into the heart of it. "Campo perro" is in the end all that I can think to say.

They look back, confused. They walk on, a little disappointed, as if still none the wiser. And I know full well that my tongue refuses to roll the Rs of Spanish, and so I wonder if, and almost hope, with pleasing amusement, that I just blamed 'country pears'.

Sometimes as I ride, this couple and all the other people appear to me together. The memory of them returns and as I see each of them again it gives in me a warm feeling that the world is a kind place. When the road has been empty for a while, without a stop and only the sounds of the bicycle for company, I revisit their faces, the way they stand, their expressions, and where I found them.

I re-ride that slow incline through the misty hills of Extremadura, then down the deserted cloud-slicked cobbled streets of a 7am Sunday morning. All is shut, but for one café, which I suppose is technically also a bar because, on one small shelf, of about a single square foot, there is also a bottle of whisky. A husband and wife in masks; he at the till and coffee machine, she with a steel mixing bowl of batter and a deep fat fryer. She drops in lengths of batter that go sizzling into churros. The café is full, a throng of people. I take my place at the counter on a high stool. Beside me is a gendarme in olive green uniform, eating his churros and mixing his cocoa into warm milk as innocent as a boy. I join the men in adding milk to my normally black coffee. I do as they do; I even add sugar. I watch as they go hungrily about their work, and then I too dip my churros right to the bottom, fearlessly deep, of my glass of coffee.

There is the din of a day starting. For some reason each gold coin in payment or change is slapped down hard on the counter, like this is Vegas. People arrive with orders for their own home's breakfast table; the woman takes them, so diligently, and the golden-fried and bending rods of batter are ready in no time, wrapped in brown paper that shines with absorbing fat that turns the paper translucent as it is swept up and carried out the door. The small room is full with such a hubbub, and few are smiling but all are content, as if what happens here is the most serious of affairs, which, in a way, I suppose it is. The orders go back and forth in this morning business, of life starting on this trading floor, another bourse for the new day.

Another of these portraits in time and place: Coruche, let it be Coruche, the town in the interior of Portugal with nothing bigger than the bull ring and the vain efforts of officials and businesses in Lisbon and Porto to have people relocate to places like it.

The waitress slides down my bowl of soup on another damp morning. In the bowl is the orange of pumpkin that has vanished from its form. There are a few stems of green leaf, flaking but not quite broken apart. Over her mask, she smiles with her eyes. She wears those pearl earrings, humbly elegant, or flash but somehow not, because all the women of Iberia seem to wear them, having had their ears pierced in infancy and keeping the same pearls right through to old age, so that by their normalcy they look as plain as a cloth apron. The eyes smile at me again, with a beauty that is also somehow sad, as if in the look there is held also a great deal of thought, of concern for this world. She asks if I would like anything more with my food, and I think I would like, with this world right now so tender and so fragile, to tell her that she is beautiful, but this seems a lot, and so I just ask for the pepper instead.

She returns, places down the mill with another smile of pure kindness. I ask if she is from Coruche. Yes. How is it? It is fine. Small...but close to bigger places. I nod across to the bull ring. People just come for the bullfights, tourism? She shrugs. Yes. Some. But our bull fights are different. The tone of her voice demurs, like she is not that kind of person. Likes animals. Here the bull does not get killed in the ring. Not like Spain? Si. Exacto. Not like Spain. She goes on, says:

"It is a good place," as if this realisation about bulls improves her estimations of her town.

And then she says that most simple, timeless of things. "It is a good place to bring up our children."

I smile at the smiling eyes, as she prepares to leave but first asks again. "Is there anything else?"

And again I want to tell her that she is beautiful, in case it is long since she felt it, in case the weight of the world is on her also. But it is not my place, and so I shake my head and hope she feels it, or the lightness of it, and a final time I smile at the smiling eyes. And she is gone.

A last portrait then, one I found some five hundred kilometres ago and have ridden with from just beyond the yellow birch in central Spain; Guadalupe. Beneath the stone walls of that monastery the size of a castle, with its steeples and its spires, its tiles of metal atop them, blues and yellows and Gaudi green diamonds slotting together. Grand oak doors and archways, long windows, turrets; pure fairy tale glory rising into the mist in this anonymous mountain village I've never even heard of. I sit beneath the monastery in its splendour, I drink my coffee, as if the splendour were only a condiment to the coffee, a sort of visual sweetener. I write into a notepad and an old man in a flat cap and cane is watching me write, attentively, with a certain warmth. Like perhaps the world isn't so bad as he'd been thinking, as he goes on living his life in chronic pain and cable news.

For a while I feel him watching me. Finally I look round at him, and together, we smile.

CHARITY

INTO THE DARK SHADE of a restaurant; blinds are down, shift over.

On the bar a silver platter with the remains of saffron yellow paella rice and the red-pink and shattered shell of a langoustine. In the heavy shadow it all looks baroque; a Caravaggio, the flash of light in the steel platter its chiaroscuro. The staff look like family, gathered together at food. This is the end of their own meal after serving others; the father crosses himself with thanks to the food, looks up to see a stranger. They have all been smoking, with no effort to conceal it, though presumably here, indoors, it is against the law. The moist, pink rind of a finished watermelon is their ashtray, full with grey dust and bent, extinguished cigarette butts.

They express looks of remorse in response to my question of whether food is over. They can fix me tomato and bread, which is always good enough, and five minutes later, seated outside, it arrives to me with a small caña of beer. The tomato, pulped and pasted in, glistens red and olive oil-golden, depending on how the sunlight hits it to cut the colour.

Before I leave, I go inside to pay. A daughter asks a euro-fifty, meaning that even in a small Spanish village, often cheap, they must have given me either the beer or the bread for free. Out of change, I hand a ten euro note, at which she looks amiss. Anything smaller? In a pocket I find a euro coin, then a ten, twenty. That's it. She shakes her head, takes the note as the father looks up, asks:

"How short is he?"

"Thirty."

"It's good."

And he looks at me with a nod, sucking food out of the inside of his cheeks. He gives a smile, just barely, and the wave of a patriarch passing pardon. Something in the act, small though it is, is pregnant with kindness, one that goes beyond the thirty cents, as if he also impresses a feeling, a nurturing, upon me. The kindness seems to increase with the national alarm level. Go well, be well; this is how you repay me. His face says it solemnly from over the golden chain and the chest hairs shooting out his collar.

Next morning, I will buy manchego and tomato, to make a sandwich of the bread that I didn't eat at the restaurant the night before. The man in the shop is dressed in a white surgeon's coat in which he slices cheese and meat. After I pay, moving to the door, he picks up a baguette to go with my purchases.

"And this?" he says. "Very delicious."

"No, gracias. Yo tengo, I have."

"No. For you," he insists, just handing me the baguette. "No money."

VALENCIANA

I KNOW THAT, as I move beyond Valencia, here begins my final quarter. The city is closed-down, and so I will not enter it, but keep to the hills above as this night passes. Because it is the final quarter, it is the one that will go fastest. It is, I confess, also the most unnerving, because I don't know what follows it, just as none of us knows what follows this time we were placed into, before which we were so used to the idea that we had control of our lives.

Out of the countryside, nearing the city and its larger towns, rats begin to replace the larger roadkill – the wildcats and dogs. I suppose this is because the larger roadkill had been the predators that killed the rats, and in turn lived from them. Now the rats are all that's left for the cars.

From the last forested mountains I move, and, for just a kilometre or so, I ride high up enough to see all the way to the city; the glowing orange diamond of Valencia; streets and buildings, a map in light and butted-up hard against the Mediterranean now sheer black. As I go, I move through bars of temperature; fronts shifting ice to warm to ice, sometimes obviously corresponding to a dip in the road, a trough where mist collects, or a north-facing bend that never knew sun.

I ride the old National Highway III, one of those routes useful to cyclists because they plot a direct course between notable places, with a good surface, but have since been made obsolete by the vast construction that sucked all the cars from it, and now carries the traffic over my head. National Highway III follows, albeit humbly, the same route as the modern autovia that was built above, or blasted and cut through, all the contours I now ride up, down and around. I pedal alongside the colossal highway, falling on a trajectory as perfect as a parachutist to earth. Mesmerised, I look up; the columns of concrete so high, so far above the forest, like the tallest of trees, like straight white bones in some vast rib cage, carrying the road as it slopes towards Valencia. Headlamps go sinking down the mountainside, all with that same slow roar as I pedal through forest beside it, a road that slices clean at the mountain, some terrifying guillotine of time.

What next? Every so often and though I try not to, I cannot help but ask myself. Those words are a curse on our generation and era, though sometimes, perhaps now, warranted. I am not afraid, because what use is fear? But I am unsure, and perhaps that is every bit as unsettling.

Things begin to blur, to melt. The road winds, takes me with it, into itself; it shows me its shadows. All that waits between me and Barcelona now is coast, which has that useful habit of reminding us of the infinity of things greater than ourselves, and by it lending a certain peace to our movement through this world. This, I realise, was the opposite of the mood I had on leaving the Atlantic, but now time has worked its way back round, as it always will, for nothing lasts forever.

Sometimes as I ride, my eyes and face feel so tired, and so warm, and I wonder if it's only sleeplessness or something more. And for just a moment I shut my eyes to see what it's like, and for a moment it's good to be gone, like the whole world passing gently, like I'm ready and it's my time. Then I open them again; to that moon and forest and mountain all rolling, and it's all too beautiful.

STRANGERS

I NEVER LIKED SLEEPING in hotels. First of all, I never had the money for them. More than that, though, I always felt that once I was over that threshold I was in the transaction and that was that. I had ceded control to the proprietor. It was only by sleeping outside that I could remain in the world at all times, and that was what I wanted most of all.

In the orchard I sleep, then sleep lightly, and then am awake. Waking to a sound, a presence; regular footfall. I pull my head out of my sleeping bag. I see a man, back to me and having strode right by my feet and into the bush. Purposeful, must've seen me. Must've just let me be.

"Why is this man striding through the undergrowth on the outskirts of town in the middle of the night?" I ask myself.

I look around. I lift up on my elbow, concerned. But no; he was alone, and now he is gone.

It is not until next morning that I realise the equal and maybe greater question the universe was asked in that moment, by another voice:

"Why is this man sleeping under a tree in the undergrowth on the outskirts of town in the middle of the night?"

I suppose it is an evolutionary mechanism we have adopted; a cognitive bias that tells us that what we are doing is normal and does not need questioning, because we profess ourselves to be of sound mind. We indulge our own eccentricities but cannot be sure of the same in others, and so we doubt them, for our own safety. We are at an advantage in life, on the other hand, if we do not doubt and question ourselves. Only, however, up to a point.

DAWN RAID

PERFECT COLOURS come through silhouettes of the orchard trees; the last leaves fallen and now pruned right back close for winter. The night sky is still blue, but that rust red lifts on its eastern edge, beginning to burn in orange as sun comes up. I drink it in, but then loud, real loud cr-crackcr-cr-crack-cr-crack. From nowhere, peace is gone and there is a volley of gunfire striking right overhead and echoing all around the dawn. Men call out and beat through scrub nearby. Perhaps this is sport, perhaps only for the pigeons I saw roosting overhead. Perhaps, and I think most likely, it is pest control, for all those stray and wild dogs that again barked the whole night through.

Reasons, however, are immaterial, while my body and bullets are material. I have no desire to wait around and find out. On one level I feel my privilege, my passport and its protection; that this gunfire in the night is not meant for me, and the worst thing that will harm me here is a horrible accident. Experience – or news – of it is the worst trauma I or loved ones will have to deal with. This thought, too, however, is for another time, is for the future. I get towards my feet as more gunfire goes off, then stay low and wait, adrenaline all through me. I do not want to sit it out; but I have no wish to be a moving object in a bush, with people looking for moving objects to shoot.

The gunfire and shouts continue to ring out; I rummage in a bag for something, wondering if anything other than escape can help me. I find my head torch, and to be seen is normally the opposite of what I want, but artificial light moving around is the one thing I have that will signify human, will signify 'Don't shoot!' I stick it on my forehead; full beam. Nobody ever heard of a stray dog nor wild bird with a torch. Artificial light will get me out of here, identify me as human.

Not a target, I repeat, not a target.

The shaft of white strobes with my head as I pack hurriedly, the light illuminating all it falls upon, falls upon sleeping bag, luggage bag, shoes. Falls upon Miles, up with a creak. Falls upon orchard and wheels pushing through trees. Falls upon road, white lines, and up in the dawn, we're riding again.

INSIDES

As I RIDE, the gunshot stays with me. These days it seems everyone has trauma, everyone has Mental Health. The pandemic will bring new concerns; being shut inside like this, however comfortable and secure those insides were, will leave us new explanations for our new trauma.

I have no right to speak of trauma and yet I'm sure some of it has rubbed off on me. It is not my trauma, I would never claim that. But I've heard enough from other people that maybe I accumulated a little of theirs. That old Afghan man, curled up on the sofa of a squatted hotel in Athens. The Yemeni man in the canteen. The women who at first will not speak or even really look at a man, at me.

Back in the city, too, everyone has their own, smaller, Post-Traumatic Stress Disorder now. They have been told of it by their therapist, have learned about PTSD. It is as if all life became a battleground. On one hand I want people to experience and so process, heal, their harms. But I want them to help others do the same, to believe they can change the world away from one that harms so many as a matter of course.

I remember a banker explaining to me that the algorithms used by banks to recognise patterns in stock market movements, and to make trades accordingly, were innovated first from defence industries; from software used to recognise physical patterns and movements on the ground and target bombs accordingly. Why do we call them 'defence industries' or 'ministries of defence' when most of what they do is attack?

I remember an aid worker, one of those professional humanitarians with a good salary, who had since become a motivational speaker, teaching how her experience of refugee camps and conflict zones could help manage a modern workplace and its stresses. And I wondered why a modern workplace had come to resemble a conflict zone?

But, more than that, I wondered why there was more attention and value given to making the workplace a more manageable conflict zone, than was given to repairing the conflict zone itself, or not creating new ones, or not arming those who make new ones?

Perhaps the stresses inside the modern head are simply because we know the conflict zones and the refugee camps exist out there. That all life has become a battleground. When marketing clothes or news or policies at consumers: we are the target audience, we are the target voter, we are the target.

A truth: language is never accidental.

And in our sterile office suites, seeking only paper profits while the world outside is burning, the constant awareness of what lies beyond, swirling out of all control, induces a panic too much to bear.

Once, on a boat from Samos towards the Greek mainland, amongst a group of young Syrian men, I met a Palestinian boy. He was by far the youngest of the group he had tagged along with, and he said nothing, and the older boys seemed to have grown annoyed by him. We sat together at the back of the boat, me and this Palestinian boy, who had been made a refugee by a state we consider an ally, and so we think of him less a refugee and more as an externality, one to be kept off of the moral balance sheet. Together, the boy and I went watching the boat's disappearing swell, and saying nothing.

I still remember his slight, skinny body; his legs in jeans a bit too long because they had presumably been donated; his feet up on the rail of the boat. I remember how small he seemed, how old his eyes looked in his young face, and how now and then he looked round my way, checking on something I did not know. Unlike some of the older boys, he never said a word, only that his family – some seventy years after Israeli settlers first blazed into Palestine – were still in refugee camps near Jenin. There are some who do not speak, who say nothing because their story is still a life and not a story. Sometimes this is because they do not want to be defined by it, they are still battling it themselves and insist on their dignity above all else. Other times this is because – for them – there is nothing left to say. They have seen too much.

But I remember him more clearly than any who did talk about themselves, who were still enough in control to tell a story, or had hope enough to want to.

We hear sometimes, warmly, of the refugees and immigrants who design software, start companies, discover vaccines to viruses. These refugees will always exist, if only by the law of averages that sees 90% of the world's population kept locked-out of the world's wealth and freedom of movement, but regardless makes-up 90% of the world's population and so holds 90% of the world's talent.

That young boy, who had fled Israel's destruction of his Palestine; I do not think he will ever discover a vaccine, probably never go to university, perhaps never even learn much of the native language where he settles. But still, he has a right to be, to a home and a life after the one he had taken from him, to be supported as he builds it; beautiful as he is.

In truth, it is not the suffering I have struggled to witness, so much as the indifference to it when I am home.

*

THE INDUSTRY

ADVENTURE, I SENSE, IS PASSING. How would anybody justify taking an unnecessary journey again? For a number of years, people already talked of the adventure sector, the adventure industry. Nobody seemed to realise the significance of using these words to describe what had always been intended as the crack in the system through which the light got in. Adventure became only the valve on the pressure cooker nobody liked.

Even before the pandemic it had been struggling; collapsing under the white, Western guilt of how ridiculous it was to fly half across the world to ford a flooding river in gaiters, while Sudanese men carrying their lives in bin bags did the same in Slovenia, trousers rolled-up and hoping to make Italy, or whichever country from which they would not be pushed back towards whatever they were escaping. Adventure was just a momentary dabbling in the sense of what it is to have nothing. Adventure was temporary, voluntary hardship.

If there was a politics in adventure too, then the pandemic had laid it bare. Adventure was intended as the high point of individual liberty, the freedom to choose and to deviate, rooted in an idea of the sanctity of our lives and our own decisions. From those adventures, those efforts in exceptionalism, a little of that sanctity was supposed to trickle down; to help us test or define the limits of what it was to be human back in everyday life. So why was sanctity so hard to find? Had adventure failed, had we failed to have adventures, or had the lessons of adventure failed to make their way back to the way we ran our world?

Perhaps adventure, the industry, had simply grown bigger, while adventure, the spirit, had grown smaller. Adventure had been knotted into a world where all was humdrum, where adventure helped you get ready for work, where even a long adventure, a sabbatical perhaps, was proven to aid staff retention and loyalty over time. A world with no need of the sacred.

There was no doubting that adventurers, since I'd first been called one, had also gone mainstream. Adventure had been, as some liked to call it 'democratised'; something which, often and sadly, meant only that it had been put up for sale. Adventure had grown into the seasonal branding exercise of a department store. It had become an aftershave. A car. A wristwatch. A three-piece luggage set with a map printed on it. It was any number of physically and spiritually exhausted corporate employees paying over the odds for a prolonged and – by most measures – uncomfortable holiday in order to feel briefly alive again.

A friend in London, disillusioned with a job that paid well in return for his soul, had told me of a particularly bad week. Come Thursday evening, he'd thought "fuck it", and got a plane that night to Morocco for a long weekend of surfing lessons and sun. Come Monday, he felt OK back at the desk. I never said that here was no rebellion – there was in fact no fuck it – but only the prudent allocation of a little of his vast amounts of disposable capital, committed to a lavish and global economy of experience, so that he was rested and able to return to work next week. His boss would have been delighted.

In the past year I had seen an adventure in which a group of women had flown to Africa to pick up plastic waste on the beach. A million litres of kerosene jet fuel for expensively educated white people to go and pick up rubbish in the sun. Whatever the virtue, the good intention; as far as allocation of resources went – it was questionable.

This adventure creates a world of two places: out there – a place where we had the life we wanted – and in here, where we didn't, and more than that, could never expect to. The distant beach is where we make the changes we give-up on at home.

Others have sold the idea of adventure, but with out there/in here defined temporally:

"We know about the nine-to-five. But what about the five-to-nine?"

The idea was to leave the office and head for the hills, to the countryside after work, to sleep a night and refresh, and return to office next day. But why, I thought, had we conceded so much? Forty hours a week for forty years? This adventure was only rebellion on the boss's terms. It was adventure outside of working hours. It was to take the thing that had dreamt of changing systems, and instead put it to work, for the system.

And if it was, more innocently, just a 'fix' of adventure, that only demanded the question: Why were we broken?

CATALUÑA

MEDITERRANEAN

I PUSH THE BICYCLE through the sand; its wheel sinks a rail, a track, and it rides it to the sea. I step into the Mediterranean, having stepped out of the Atlantic I am not sure how many days ago. Iberia and a 120 euro bicycle I named Miles are all that separate the two.

There are fewer waves in the Mediterranean. The water feels cold, but my skin remembers the temperature that came in the ocean before it, and so by comparison it is mild. I stand to my knees, cool, and then drop in for my baptism: it floods over me, the temperature of the sea takes the temperature of my body, rushes one towards the other, like blue hitting red in two splashes of paint.

And I float on my back and look up towards the blue sky, I smile for a while. Back under I go, pulling myself down to the shallow seabed, the water so much more still and clear than that moody Atlantic. Beneath the water, I pick up handfuls of sand in my fingers, watch the bubbles flood as water fills the air pockets I've disturbed, and I throw forth the sand in front of me to explode in a little eternity.

SHORE LEAVE

BACK ON SHORE A MAN STROLLS up and down; cupping his hands to his breast, striking himself in the culmination of some exercise routine. A baseball cap is over his forehead and eyes, large belly shining in the sun. Buddha. A young boy runs out of the sea, stark naked, his untesticled penis shrivelled in a chrysalis, waiting to grow into patriarchy. The boy's mother goes to him with a towel and wraps her arms around him, like the towel were a cape and he is her superhero.

I wonder what the patriarchy will look like by the time this boy becomes a man. Sometimes I think we near a changing patriarchy, where the women will increasingly become breadwinners and the men stay home and bake bread. I welcome and fear the change in equal measure; the idea of women staffing an unaltered system, with the language of feminism put to the marketing of patriarchy. Or perhaps, hopefully, the realisation that, as in so many ways, here was a system that had made few happy.

The sea now is empty, full only of blue. I see the dock cranes of Valencia south and of Sagunto north. The fuel domes of a refinery stand in stripes a little up the coast, there to remind me of industry, of carbon, where all immediately around me is family, is nature. A necessary evil I suppose. From my bag I take an orange, a final free gift from nature before I visit the restaurant opposite. I slice it, quarters. I suck out its flesh and its juice, in a world and moment so bountiful.

After everything, in the end it is not so complex. Before I take my seat at a table out front of the restaurant, I already know what I will do. The sun is bright and warm and so I will order a full bottle of white wine to myself. I will begin with a plate of fried calamari. I will almost certainly have three courses, and perhaps also an espresso. Already now, and throughout it all, I will be conscious of the joy that is this honest extravagance, unthinkable in my twenties, and still now never taken for granted. As I wait on my food, I will vow to myself that should ever I earn well enough that the luxury of such extravagance is dulled, I will give away my money so that others might appreciate the same luxury, and until I learn to appreciate it properly once more. Without forsaking others, get yourself safe, and then get others safe too. This has been my working logic of a life plan for a while now. I am not yet safe, but I'm getting closer.

At my table I drink my wine; shining young, green-yellow in the sun. At the next table a couple in roller-skates eat, rolling their wheels on the feet under their chairs. A man walks by, singing to himself and his hand planted firmly on the shoulder of his wife a step ahead of him, a grip that looks possessive but I think is only affectionate, and she too smiles as if this clutch at her shoulder was all she wanted from life. A young girl rides circles of a bandstand on her bicycle. Just beyond the restaurant, under an ornamental timber frame, are two well-groomed poodles pulling at the leashes on which they are tethered, one with its tongue lolling ecstatically out as it stares into the asshole of the other. A man strides by on the beach, power walking in sunglasses and body-warmer. A boy runs, pulling at a kite.

I eat my food, watching all life walk by. Restaurants, unlike hotels, I have always found time for; for good food is the essence of a life lived properly, and should cost money, where the best places I ever slept, on the other hand, with shooting stars through the ceiling, cost nothing. Even in a bad restaurant, still I cannot blame the food itself, and must be thankful to it, if only for the calories that will take me to my next rest, and perhaps a better meal.

The waves on the beach lap onwards and the wine drifts up to my head, softening just enough. Out at sea I watch a freighter in shadow, a pair of sailing yachts on an empty water. Men fish from a rocky outcrop, that universal and timeless law where men seek cheap protein to feed a family. I remember the Vietnamese families of New York State who had done likewise, though unaware of the pollutants in the Hudson fish, ingested from fire retardants General Electric once dumped into the river. But that was a different adventure, a different time.

Across the beach, a middle-aged man does push-ups in the sand. At the next table a young girl, bored with her family, holds two phones and sings a song; one phone photographs the two poodles, the other in front of her face records her voice. And it is strange to think how many of the earth's resources have been enlisted in a thing so simple as a child's song.

NIGHT TO BENICARLO

SOMETIMES, I CONSIDER how many millions of places I've been to only once, passed through and then left forever never to return. They've all been kind to me, really, each in its own different way.

The evening lowers flat down upon me. The municipal lights are on a dodgy circuit that now and then settles the street into darkness for a minute or two, before illuminating again. From the church opposite, doors of buttressed oak are flung back and open to welcome any hesitant worshipper. A scaffold supports the atrium in its renovation, beneath which the priest in white coat throws out his arms to deliver mass. I ride through those small towns with nothing in them, where the older teenagers sit together outside the one bodega, where nothing ever happens, and conspire how to one day leave. Eventually they will get out, and then, eventually, they will return to resolve that, all along, it was home.

Two Arab men talk business, one tapping at a notepad as he leans against the business premises, which is only their white van with a picture of fruits and vegetables, and the contact details of their fruit and vegetable wholesale. An old couple who run the pharmacy sit laughing on the front step under the light of their green cross, offering its own version of salvation beneath the church. I watch, I watch and take it all in. This is here, this is everywhere, this was the world, this was my world; I just shared it here and for a little while. Again, I ask myself if I've got to stop living like this, or if by now it's the only way I know how to live.

The main highway sits above me as I ride, it runs beneath the hills and a white church glowing high on top of the mountain that guards the coast. My own road is below and lined by mostly closed businesses, and I feel something about more closed truck stops has trepidation in it; those places that never shut, that were always lit even on a dark highway, and now here, shuttered, dusked. The menu is still there from the last normal day, before everything. Sardines.

The trucks themselves are still going, which makes some sense as without the truck stop I suppose by definition a truck cannot stop. On the elevated road overhead, around the hillsides, one after the next come the blocks of orange light along truck undercarriages, as if the things float over the road and make their way like sleds raced through night. The mist. Damn but the mist is heavy. Cloud all the way down. The onion dome on the Church of Magdalena de Pulpis glows like a firefly, the bell tolls in the belfry, on the hill they call La Serra d'Irta.

Up ahead I see blue light, cops pulled in. I ride on, remembering the armed police I already saw at the Catalan frontier. Cataluña, as Scotland back home, I feel in its public health policy has also an agenda to differentiate itself in daily life from the state it means to break from. I check my pocket for a mask just in case, as the blue lights near slowly. Closing in, I see an orange wand, waving traffic; a car pulled over, lights on full and hazards too. I get close, I see faces. They want nothing from me, but then a cop in a ponytail she calls at me in alarm, an alert that draws my attention to her just when it needs to be – Shit! – I swerve. Snout and bristling whiskers split open and a slug of brain nerve all down the road. Boar. But credit to him, he's written-off the whole fucking car on his way out, just like they always do. The same thing once happened to a friend, driving back through deepest Brittany, waking from sleep to the one word of her boyfriend, said quiet and foreboding, before the car totaled. "Sanglier". A huge shadow in the headlights, and then bang.

I ride on, shake cool air into my head, revive my senses but damn this night is weird. Olive trees meet forest all around, and so much mist envelopes everything, high up as we are and in that heady feeling of altitude. Ahead are two eyes, fireflies, green eyes; no, dog eyes. Bounding for me out the forest. I make tall, make brave, but the creature is small, it whimpers and I realise it is not coming for me. He smells hot blood, hog blood, and the happy hound pads on back down the road towards the kill, tongue out. I ride on through the mist, another shape appearing in the hard shoulder: Fox. Dead fox. Carrion. How did so much wind-up dead here? Was it the moon, the full moon of yesterday that dragged the animals out their dens and the cover of their trees, that left them all on-heat and lusting fatally towards the road? I breathe in the night and ah but it stinks, this mist so full and on which each smell lives twice. Like blood and death and cum and shit, this pungency, as if earth died screaming and all the world were being born anew tonight. I look over my shoulder and at the line of the mountains, the cardiogram. Buh-bhum, buh-bhum, buh-bhum. And I put my thumb and finger to my neck: buh-bhum, buh-bhum, buh-bhum. Still with us. We're good. Down at my feet I look, turning over pedals, like they're kicking at the night, running just above the road, just like the trucks float a little way above their highway. My dreams they collide with reality, and in the fire between the two there is a light, and close to it you hold, breathing the sweet air of life, of success and failure, and that, that savoured light, is all it takes, is all it takes to keep you on.

Briefly down towards the coast I drop, drop into the brutal industrial capacity of the tourism infrastructure. Fun away from home for the millions who haven't enough fun at home. In ziggurats, obelisks, balconies and fortified positions beneath a softly fading mountain scape, the apartment buildings line the roadside, towering over everything and yet empty as a trench. And I wonder where the leisure normally found here is to be found during this pandemic. And I wonder where that sense of escape is escaping to instead, or if it has found no other outlet, and so it waits elsewhere, bottling.

Miles? Miles? But for the first time Miles actually he sounds good, sounds like he was born for this, as back up the hills we go, and my head moves side to side and he creaks and whistles and squeals and creaks, bitches brew, like the ghosts of all the greats are dead and spinning, playing in his bottom bracket and howling at the chain. A drum, a cymbal, a snare, a drum. A drum, a cymbal, a snare, a drum…our brains find music in repetition, and damn, but right now Miles is playing everything clear off the stage. Virtuoso, doesn't give a damn just fucking creaks, like the world is tearing up in half but still he'll move forward. But still he will move forward. A light idles side-to-side from my head torch, and I grunt with the sound of the chainring and the whistle of the crank bolt slowly shearing itself free of this world like a spirit leaves its body. The moon cuts shapes at the clouds that pass, a wind presses with the sound of a train, and there are no stars tonight, and there are no stars tonight.

WILD FRUIT

DOWN A LANE a pomegranate tree is giving meaning to its name: apple grenade. Overripe, the things explode on their branches with a thousand tiny parcels of crimson. An old couple are on-hand and sampling one fruit, burst and scarlet, that they have picked. Others they have pulled down are waiting to be tried, stacked on the edge of an irrigation canal. "It's good?" I ask. He considers, savouring, a connoisseur of these camino trees, a sommelier waiting for the notes on his palate. Finally, he pronounces, like a court judge:

"Muis acerbo."

Too bitter.

On the edge of the orange plantation, one tree grows wild; a seed that has fallen furthest from the tree and then started a life unpruned and unshaped. I cut a fruit from its branch, knowing before my knife even slips in what this one will be like compared to all the others: more sharp, more bitter. Not grown to consumer tastes, nor to yield, nor for transportation.

Here is the orange as it was meant to be. Its original form. This orange is the truth.

At the roadside I pass beside an almond tree, with all those tapered, dotted shells beginning to blacken and soften around its trunk as the old nuts begin to rot. Rolling on and I pass something else, something beautiful and curious, in that way the roadside always is. I make a note to write it down later, but later that evening am happy to realise I've forgotten what it was. Sometimes there comes a point where even the recording in words is little better than pointing a camera; perhaps a loftier version, but born of the same place, the resolve to capture.

Just let the world be, I tell myself. Let it be.

NATION STATE

THE ROADSIDE SHOWS the politics of my new geography. I near Castillon, though the road sign has been doctored in spray paint, adding that final, Catalan N to the plain Castillo officially offered by Madrid's highways agency. Though most of the signs are bilingual, this one has missed the all-important closing letter, leaving just Castillo; the city's name according to the cultural imperialists of Castille in Madrid. I think of all those towns in Northwest China, in Uyghur, on Highway G312, and with their Turkic names made Mandarin.

The red-yellow of Cataluña appears everywhere. In every town, flags have been diligently tied to almost all of the balconies and lampposts, with a level of coverage that suggests it is an official policy, but with flags and methods of attachment – string, zip-ties, rope – that are makeshift in a way that, on the contrary, suggests this is only an organic and popular will. When the will is so popular, I wonder at what point the official policy has to meet it.

On one corner, and on the balconies of adjacent houses, is one Catalan flag and then, rare, endangered even, on the next house, a Spanish one; the Castille coat of arms, also on the same red-yellow.

I wonder how these neighbours get on, if they get on. If they are friends? I wonder if they fell out over politics, nations, Catalan independence? Or maybe they never liked one another to begin with and so married their feud about noise volume or late nights on the balcony to a meta-level, political one. I remember such stories from Yemen, where some regional tribes chose to side in the war with the Saudi state, but only out of convenience, and so that the US would come and drop bombs on the neighbouring tribe with which they already held grievance.

I look at the red-yellow of the Catalan flag and the red-yellow of the Spanish, different only with its coat of arms. I wonder how distant and indifferent to this political feud you would have to be to see only two red and yellow flags? I wonder if there is a sufficiently external group to both, perhaps sufficiently hostile to the interests of both, that the Spanish and Catalans might make common cause as simply two groups, both with red and yellow flags? Perhaps China, with its economic power and its own red and yellow flag might pose just this sort of threat, as it is increasingly seen to across Europe and the West. I wonder if a superior life form, from another planet, would be confused at why there was so much discord between the people who all found their belonging in red and yellow flags.

Under a motorway bridge, one afternoon, I see one more familiar flag; that of Turkey. Although, it is not quite that of Turkey; it has been altered to make it one more in red and yellow. The star and crescent has been put upon the flag of Spain, above the heavy portmanteau 'Turquispain'. I stop and look at it, intrigued and fearful that this country of which I am fond, Spain, is about to see fit to abuse that other country that is also dear to me. I try to make sense of the Spanish which, on reflection and verification, says that:

Sense justicia, sense democracia, Quin Fastic España?!

Without justice, without democracy, What Fascism is Spain?!

And then Turquispain, so that Spain, I suppose is like Turkey. I consider what this means. 'Like Turkey'? Do they mean it is like cups of tea on the ferry across the Bosphorus on your way to work? Do they mean good green bean dishes, particularly in autumn? Turquoise sea and beaches? Soup at 3am? Barber shop shaves with change from two euros?

I suppose, as the graffiti says, the author means 'like Turkey' as in not having justice or democracy. And yet, I wonder why the author needs a geographically remote and mostly Muslim country to make this point. Equally, as contained in the point they are making, there are political prisoners in Spain, with protests outlawed and protesters beaten. The rule of law has been suspended to jail them, and so, surely Spain is in fact, more pertinently, more relevantly, and more obviously…in fact…like Spain?

MULTIMEDIA

A STOP SIGN, on which someone spray paints the words 'the war' beneath. 'Covid Plandemic' is on concrete balustrades. Nearing the cities, the graffiti rises with the tower blocks on the horizon. This too is media, and yet it is rarely talked about as such.

The importance of a piece of writing is proportionate to the effort and risk taken to write it. Graffiti is a criminal offence. The UK is the only country in the world that is called 'developed' where you can go to jail for graffiti. A friend of mine once did, five months for spraying his art on a wall. Other artists became celebrated rather than incarcerated and, were their identity not a secret, could go to Christie's auction house instead. I'm not sure who decides whether you go to the jailhouse or the auction house.

Some of the graffiti has an obvious meaning, such as the Spanish-Turkish flag, or STOP the war. Others have meaning less obvious to me, but entirely obvious to the creator who rose in the night to put them there. The person trespassing on a railway line beside the abandoned carriage. The person on the narrow lip of that building. The person hanging beneath the motorway bridge. A few times in the Valenciana region, I see Rowan in large green bubble letters; is it my favourite tree, a local woman or man, or just a coincidence of these shared names? There are other tags that are only sequences of letters too large and compacted to detect. Then a letter and a number: D-39. Letters: ZSK. Then on the reverse of a road sign, the familiar one that always makes me smile: ACAB.

Did they put it there for me? For them? And I remember the Gypsy man, long ago outside the café in Portugal's interior, who sang only for himself.

As I cycle, I consider our groups, our tribes. I am an outsider of most everywhere I travel through. In some places, particularly the Muslim world, the emphasis on giving welcome means being an outsider can quickly see you taken right to the heart of the family, the community. The path from outside to inside is a direct one.

As I cycle, I am nevertheless an insider of the cycling tribe. In truth, so much of my life has been spent on a bicycle that I identify with being on a bicycle even when I am not. Because I grew up in a time and place where few cycled, those who did, we all nodded at one another. Now, even in places where many cycle, I still nod, but get few in return – mostly from the older riders who remember what it was like, before all this. After the weeks of pedalling all day, my cycling is now so deep inside me that, when I walk down a street, back to or away from Miles, still I give a nod at an approaching cyclist, who looks at back at me with confusion. Then I remember I am right now just a pedestrian: we do not have our vehicles in common, and our humanity alone is not enough to explain this level of affinity. I have heard the drivers of Volkswagen camper vans confess to accidentally doing the same, even after moving on to new vehicles.

Looking down at its rotations, it strikes me that the wheel of a bicycle has no sides, just as it has no beginning or end. Perhaps it is symbolic that one of humankind's most effective inventions is neither linear nor binary, and its sole purpose is moving forwards easily. Looked at differently, I suppose there are sides to the wheel; inside and outside, just as I suppose we as humans construct our in-groups and our out-groups to make sense of the world by forming belonging. Where we differ from the bicycle wheel, however, is that the perimeter of the wheel, where the outside and the inside meet, is designed and intended to have as little friction as possible at the point where it meets the outside world. One moves easily over the other.

I think of the news bulletins, which are now so relentless they are no longer truly bulletins so much as bullets; a constant artillery fire in a senseless war that numbs our feelings so actual wars with real bullets can take place elsewhere. I think of the newspaper headlines, the broadcasters that follow the newspaper headlines, headlines that were themselves approved by newspaper barons. The information signal of this structure is then dispatched to my phone in tiny segments. In it there lately seems to be talk of one word more than others; polarisation. There is apparently an intractable divide being set up between humans of different views.

Riding on, I disagree. People are typified by warmth towards one another. Or at worst – and though it is a condition in which evil can still thrive – by indifference.

I think of the term multimedia, and I think that roadsides are media; the original multimedia. The debris at them is media, the graffiti is media.

Sometimes we write of media and sometimes, with a capital letter, of Media. One media is incidental, the other Media is institutional; one is organic, the other is organised. In the same way, sometimes, people talk of small-p politics. By chance, and as with other words, a capital letter is necessary when the institution directly concerns capital; its representation, defence or, sometimes, a challenge to it.

Behind the statement that the world is polarised is a further assumption so basic that it mostly goes unsaid, and as a result is forgotten. The assumption is that that the Media describes the world as it truly is.

Both Media and Politics, along with those other entities that prosper in conditions of loneliness, are abstractions. That the Media contains the truth of the world is no more the case than the idea that the contents of a painting inside a frame shows all the world outside the frame. The contents of the bag on my bike have proven enough to live from, but it is not all of my life. I have seen the world as I cycled through Iberia, but not all of the world, and not even all Iberia. Media is a selection of the world, from which an abstraction is made and then offered out.

In Politics, likewise, all of the issues up for debate in a parliament are not all of the issues up for debate, or even considered important, in the café, in the street, in the bar, in the home. The limits of what a parliament will do in their current form will not touch even the beginnings of what the world needs. When I see the claim that the world became polarised, the abstraction of the Media is describing the abstraction of Politics, but with the sum total of two abstractions expressed as if one reality.

Abstraction + Abstraction = Truth = Reality.

I am not sure.

Across history, Media became a bigger business than its origins required. To reduce its costs, it became more reliant on opinion – which is cheaper to generate – than facts, which require computation and discovery, and so are expensive. This is not to say that a fact is only a number or statistic that must be computed. A fact is also a young Asian woman in a rural town telling you something about her life, and the lives of her friends who are also living on low-incomes and white. A fact is not only a number, most facts are not numbers.

Numbers are no more true than words, we just cling to them harder, and so increasingly the most deceitful words now go dressed in numbers. This is unfortunate, because numbers used honestly can be crucial, and can save or better lives.

To reduce its costs, Media moved into larger but fewer and more centralised offices. Local newspapers, the reporters at my roadsides, they died, and when they left, they took with them a granular view of the world, leaving their industry ever more reliant on abstractions, on categorisations, to describe the world from the offices.

Without granular media, firm categories became more salient; race, gender, sexuality. Class also becomes salient, but because it is harder to define, and because the Media is drawn mostly from one class, it is talked about less, and often inaccurately. Sometimes, educational attainment becomes a substitute, a cipher, for class. Sometimes a thing so arbitrary as an accent becomes the cipher. The abstraction becomes a layering of ciphers, one on top of the other, in the aim, which really is more of a hope, of building truth. With each cipher, a little more is lost. Media describes the categories, because they are obvious, but obscures the common class interest, because it is granular, less convenient to discuss, and because the owners of the Media do not want it discussed. It is the poverty of information in the separate categories of Media that have driven them further apart, into a state of conflict that has little bearing on the population.

Last of all, in the constant provision of information, both fact and fiction, and in the commodification of our attention, the Media was left to compete. In particular it was left to compete with the world of entertainment; to compete for our time and for our loyalty. The consumer of news becomes ever more a customer; the paper is a movie ticket no longer made of paper.

At this point, with a customer and an audience, narratives become useful. Tribalism, plot, and the added intensity of a struggle between light and dark; good and evil.

Sometimes the use of a little-known word is only a pretentiousness that obscures clear understanding. But sometimes it is useful to give something its precise name, so that you know when you are being asked to believe in it, and to help us describe quickly and simply when something is wrong. The word for a world in supposed eternal conflict between good and evil is Manichean. The word comes from the religion of the third-century Iranian prophet, Mani, which centred a struggle between light and dark.

A two-party political system, or a voting system that makes one inevitable, also has the potential to polarise, to become

Manichean. One party can become good and the other bad, with a different opinion depending who you ask. As such, Media and Politics can have a shared interest in a Manichean view of the world. This is also a problem if the two parties are in fact quite similar.

So what does it mean, when the Media says we are polarised? Is it simply wrong? Perhaps it helps to examine not the claim but the claimant? Could it be that we are not seeing a polarised world so much as a polarised Media? An establishment that has been impoverished of deep, granular learning or information, and which in its place has become more reliant on a retail model of information, where belonging, loyalty, and a sense of in-groups and out-groups are integral to the retail-offer. We see a polarisation in Media that is matched also by its increased dislocation from the world it seeks to describe. One solution is certainly to pay more for media, but then the reader becomes ever more the customer, who already knows that they want, and has the habit of always being right, which is a problem if they are wrong.

I ride on, the rubber of the road is humming its tune. I am nearly at my goal. The wind is at me and it is loud in the trees. Litter lines the roadside; some bags, a rotten banana skin on the asphalt, yellow and brown. It is messy, but it is real. I used to see the ribbon of tape cassettes all down these roadsides, and these days it is gone. This missing media by its absence reports faithfully on the digitalisation of classical music, pop albums, plays, book readings, the playlists our friends made for us.

Graffiti returns. Someone has written, in Spanish and in English, in spray paint, Cataluña is *not* Spain; Castillon is *not* Spain. And someone has then visited with their own spray paint to cover and erase the words not, thus reclaiming Cataluña for Madrid, at least in the terms of this highway contract written on a concrete wall. Others, elsewhere have written anti-Nazi, only to see racists remove the anti using their own spray paint. Likewise, their fascism has been given by its opponents a new anti.

Not only is the roadside granular, it also has a sense of humour the internet will always struggle to match. The internet is a digital contraption; and so, in its makeup it has to be coded in the binary noughts and ones that activate its circuit boards. The roadside is not binary, and so it cannot be Manichean. Though it is linear, I think the roadside might be the least binary thing in the world, for it shows you everything. The Internet is binary, and so Manichean outcomes are resting in its being.

In addition to the limitation of being binary; the internet page is finite, while the world in fact is infinite. Each page is telescopic, while the world is panoramic. On the internet, every page is settled, while the world is contested.

At the roadside, a poster of a fascist far-right party has been pasted up, but so too has someone attempted to peel it away, and so too has someone drawn a moustache and horns on the face of the so-called politician. This image of triumphant fascism cannot be our destiny, because in itself it is contested; a reminder that the destiny is in the contestation.

TO TARRAGONA

THE LAST OF IT, the endings; they come to all of us, and to all rides, eventually.

The earth has been put to work. Dust and shit is everywhere. A mountain is blown open beside it, the preheaters and kilns, the blast furnace of a cement factory. Cemex. Conveyor belt across the road and onto a dock for waiting boats. Everything is cement-slicked, the olive trees all terrified, cowering, covered in cement dust like old Italian clowns beneath volcanic ash out of Vesuvius. Offshore I see aquaponics, rings of sea creatures, kept and stinking in the density in which they are grown for shipping and sale.

Down the coastal road the dump trucks all drag their own dust trails up out of the cart tracks, as if dust itself is the cargo being delivered. Tractors harrow at dry fields, throwing up dust still more as there arrives the smell of shit where manure is spread. Farmers slash and burn at old crop and brush, smoke chokes at me.

In the exploitation of land and mineral all through this hinterland, so too come the prostitutes, the sex workers; that feature of the economies of Southern Europe and their kilometre-intensive manufacturing characteristics, where directors drive Audis and workers trucks but all have one thing in common, moving with them between the sites where the economy is built, signed-off, shipped. Two women talk, one leaning on the arm of the other. They flash smiles at me, each with her own chair; offices a hundred metres apart but meeting a moment in the same office to parley. One woman has a lounge chair, high arm rests; talk show host style, tell me your problems. The other is on a high chair, more the gameshow, a perch for the foot in this land of opportunity.

The land opens, the river comes – Ebro – widening as a serpent for this, delta country. Rivers and reeds, that pure colour of green banks to bright blue water beneath long bridges onto which trucks thunder, that same hammer as they cross the metal brace from terra firma to bridge platform. I pedal across, looking down at sheer water so far below, where the rising sea level encroaches steadily on the silt and its delta habitat. With a thick head, tired from so much moving, from such little sleep, I fear that I am too spent to feel and so describe this waterworld as it deserves, and Miles and his growing noises take too much of my attention.

Tarragona beckons. Freight, all freight thunders on rails. I see canvas-hooded wagons, commodity pilgrims dressed in cassocks; a vintage in this world of intermodals bearing shipping containers and fuel tanks. An all-but empty commuter train roars through the narrow passage quarried for it from the rock above the sea. The rails they gleam and roll, through refineries with their old and labyrinthine stacks, their catalytic cracking that different densities of oil and vapour and naphtha condensate rise up through. The chimneys, the fuel tanks, those domed holds, petroleum mosques stamped Repsol-Repsol-Repsol. I watch the train lines, I watch all of them; watch the high speed intercity as it glides, the regional as it cries, and then, most blessed of all and just as I am moving beyond the yard and its tracks, the freight as it clatters with that old sound: Maersk-Maersk-Maersk.

The road heads on, heads on, and the traffic grows on the tarmac in to Barcelona. Trucks in particular thunder all too close, with the same old hammer blow of that air they displace, the roar of the air in their undercarriage. All this I have by now grown used to, but still, I shake my head, my little human irritation, so small and undetectable beneath their mechanical force.

To ride a bicycle, I think and not for the first time, perhaps above all things is to know vulnerability. For sure, there are the bankers on expensive carbon fibre machines, rushing to work to short the Ethiopian rice harvest. But sometimes I think, even they, even they must get it. The bicycle is how sometimes even wealthy white men have come quite well to understand the nature of power and vulnerability. Because, to be on a bicycle in certain kinds of traffic is to glimpse quite often the small difference between living and dying, which makes our spirit cling to living, and so realise the value of our life, and so the value of all life. On a bicycle, even the wealthy and the privileged can come to gain empathy for the wretched, who should not have to face such threats to their lives and livelihoods, but nevertheless do.

The words 'should not' are important. It is not that on a road there are not rules to protect the cyclist – there are. But this, if anything, is the crucible of the realisation; the fact that the rules do not protect you. The rules are to be broken with impunity and one of those broken rules may take you with it. Often, just like the brave fiddler crab in Coruche, it will not be malice by which you are harmed, oh no, it will be only the complete and total indifference of the road system to your existence in it. The system, in fact, does not work, and the system does not work to protect the vulnerable. It should not be this way – indeed there are laws saying it should not be – but it is, and so; now what?

Once you have seen this reality in one system, even something as basic as a road system; once you have known what it is to be vulnerable, you can begin to see it in other systems. You begin to imagine what it is for others to be vulnerable too, and to accept that other systems might also be flawed.

Let me also tell you though, that this vulnerability, as I ride, and perhaps also as you ride, is not only a negative one.

To ride is to know that you were vulnerable, but because you loved to ride, you would take that risk.

It is to say that you would not have it any other way, that you could not live any way but free.

And so, in the midst of this vulnerability, is a great and towering strength; a power, like that of the protester who knows they will not return the baton strike of the cop, because the force of the cause in which they have faith will eventually repel it, long after the ache of the blow has faded.

To ride is just what you had to do, and by exercising those rights that anyway were inviolably yours, you came gradually to will them into being.

Once in a while, you pass others who are doing the same thing.

And together, contesting destiny, you make destiny.

VILANOVA I LA GELTRÚ

AN OLD WOMAN HUMS, familiar bars; familiar at least to people of a certain generation the world over, maybe meaningless to many ears of my own generation, maybe unheard to those younger. She hums bars of music from a film, bars from before the time when the world schismed, broke into an infinite supply of different bespoke cultures and information systems; when a Hollywood studio made a film, and that was that for the entire planet. Monolithic systems have upsides as well as down, as we all sit here, each within our own silo.

With feeling she hums this old tune, like it means something to her just as it does me, as she goes leaning beside her car with a couple of other silhouettes. Hummm-hum hum-hum hummm. In my head, I hear the words of a song, 'Somewhere Over the Rainbow', that my mother and sister sang once in a lullaby, now long ago, to soothe her as my grandmother, she from the heart of that twentieth century, and who had loved that film, died from cancer in a hospital bed.

The headlights of cars move along a road way below, skirting the edge of the cliff; journeys ending, journeys beginning, and the sea turning black to churning white beside the waves, winding and unwinding around the rocks to leave reels of flickering film in an old cinema.

Edged with darkness, we move on, waiting for either night to deepen or day to dawn, depending how you look at it. The road runs through and turns around a cliff face, where columns of concrete hold the mountain up above the tarmac, breaking the world into frames. A pigeon bursts above, wings flap and then pull back, as if it sprung from a magician's hat, before slowing the descent into a hole where it nests inside the rock. A few remaining clouds move on, sky clears, and the pale green lights that mark the ends of the rods of the night fishermen, they zip through the air and hover on the darkness above the water.

On the hillside a building; a man, broad shouldered, alone in an empty restaurant; his outline framed in the yellow light of the window where he sits, dead centre, wrapped in a cardigan and with his elbows up on the table, head lowered. I wonder if he is worried or only thoughtful in his solitude; a man seated at the secular altar of his mealtime. Food, I think to myself, might be both the only true secularism and perhaps the only true faith; that rare, vanishing place where you can find soul with no need of God. Towards the man I spirit my thoughts, a little of my own will, and I wonder if he will receive it; how connected we really are.

Again that question, 'what comes next?'

After the pandemic is like a shadowy cupboard, or the space behind a heavy curtain in an old house that we hesitate to pull aside. To learn without suffering first is the test and the goal of humanity, but I wonder if discovering the fragility of life, as with the deaths of a world war, will help to draw us closer, and what that might even mean.

Will we be able to look into the eyes of a stranger and see there the eyes of a loved one? Is such a thing even possible, and would that world be better or lesser for it? Would such universal love spell the end of magic, in the same way stars need the darkness of a night to shine?

Overhead the moon is full, orbited by its corona of light, glistening against another fast-passing cloud. I think of how I always loved the word, corona, how it sounded exactly like it was, and now perhaps it will be tainted and lost to us. Off to the side of the sky, Antares is burning soft and red; a dying star, a dying star. I ride under the firmament, its patchwork of time travel; dots of light, the source of some stars still burning, others already gone, their light to continue long after them; a million miles of light already shot-out, and the journey to my waiting eyes not yet nearly finished. The memory, the legacy of stars scatter the night, will outlast me and you, while down here few believe any longer in legacy, in things greater than ourselves, or in anything that can't be measured. We weep silently, we weep; counting, always counting.

This time, the journey, I tried to write it simply, so very simply. To show the world only as I found it; that world which I still cannot help but feel that we all would fall in love with, if only we could see it in such simple terms as these. The bicycle to me was only the least intrusive narrator of the world I was able to find. Travelling upon it is an aid to the final task of the writer, which is to see each human and feel, deep in your soul, and though the world often teaches us not to; here is a human, living a life, just like me.

From this point does all the magic in the universe stem.

BARCELONA

HE LOOKS AT MILES, rattles its crank, shaking back-forth in the bottom bracket. The thing is so broken you can no longer tell where. If it's the axle, the crank, the bearings. Impressively broken. He tries to shift the front gear, and though I didn't trouble to tell you, the gear mechanism sheared off on the last miles into Barcelona. The slow, noisy rub of the chain finally cut through it, and so the gear shifts nowhere. He looks at me, apologetically.

"This bicycle is only problems to me."

Ain't that the truth.

"20 euros?" I reply, already down from my 50 euros, a number that itself I had only begun with so as to enable the following 20. I point to the wheel, earnest.

"They are good tyres."

"Yes, but we have good tyres. I am sorry my friend."

I look around me. Throw it in, an auction in reverse.

"Ten euros?"

"Ten?" He replies, like what even is the point and why would I bother? But that ten it simply means that I have not been totally humiliated here, or abandoned something that once I paid money for. It is ten differences between logical and totally illogical. Perhaps this pilgrimage should've taught me not to think like this, but apparently not yet; capitalism dies hard.

He speaks Catalan to another man, who seems to be the boss. I look around at the shop: El Ciclo. It is cut from the very same cloth, or perhaps rubber, as Bina Clinica in Lisbon; an idealistic and yet practical effort at making a living. I wonder if the guys in Lisbon know the guys in Barcelona; or know of one another. Sometimes it happens that way, the community finds itself in other places; a friend passing through, or moving to a new city and looking for work.

The man and his boss look over at me. Finally, I see a nod, and, hot-damn, I think they're gonna go for it, can hardly contain my excitement as he walks back towards the counter and I'm possibly about to lose Miles and gain ten euros, which as exchanges go has about it the sense of a whole new level of wonderment.

"Yeah?" I call after him, hopefully.

"Yeah, OK." He replies.

He returns to me; six coins; four twos and two ones, dropped into my hand.

Not even a note, but who cares? Even at ten euros, the guy doesn't seem entirely happy; a final confirmation, a primitive one, communicated psychologically and silently, that I was lucky to get this deal. It was paid for with persistence.

I walk down the street where walking never felt so good. Among all the shuttered shops, bars, cafes; one is open. All the way open, bona fide open, none of that take-away tat. A few men are even inside and it seems I could even stand, resplendent, at the bar itself, by now the height of fine dining. I walk up, put my foot to the brass rail, order a coffee, a croissant from its basket. Other men are drinking beer, beer in glasses. On top of the coffee machine, glorious; ceramic cups. I wonder if he will reach for one of their handles, but he brings out a disposable and my heart sinks as he places it under the tap where coffee begins to pump and hammer out.

"Señor!" I call out, pointing up. "Ceramic! Ceramicos!... Por favor, por favor!"

And that blessed man – full with a blessed willingness to interpret law ambiguously – pulls out the disposable in the nick of time, and as the coffee begins to flow down into my ceramic, a tear of brown joy moves across white gloss.

I drink my coffee, I eat my pastry; savouring the permanence of the saucer, the firmness of a cup handle, the decency of a roof above and the solidity of a flat surface rather than the cupped palm of my hand to eat from. The owner slides down a till receipt: 2.50. I give three from the sale of Miles. Well spent, so very well spent.

On the television are protests in the United States. A president called Donald Trump has just lost the election, and crowds form with the look of vigilantes, answering his call to throw the result into disrepute. The bar in which I stand is of a certain cut. Everyone around me, with his beer in front of him before noon, looks like he drinks too much. The men all have masks under chins or hanging from one ear in a respect of authority best described, and at most, as partial. The proprietor is masked so too, though he also with an urgency that he should not be caught with any of us inside of this illicit gathering.

Watching the news, a man beside me shouts furiously. He slams his hand down firm on the bar with a bang; I look round at him; slicked back hair and eyes truly enraged, really aflame.

"Puta! Socialists!"

He screams at the victors, appearing on screen. It seems an odd charge against some of the most brazen supporters of Corporate America ever to hold office, but unmistakable is that he is enraged, unlike myself, that Trump has lost. Beyond the clear fact of his mood, he is also one of those men who seeks to invite you into his rage; he begins explaining it to me as if his rage were ordinary and obvious, as if he can maybe lessen this rage if only he can share it with someone.

Perhaps, he too holds this idea that the results are not real, just as this pandemic, the one obliging him to hold a mask under his chin, is not real, but only part of a wider conspiracy against his right to just be, to be only as he pleases. In fairness to him, the better-educated people who lost the last election in that country did much the same, only blaming Russian spies rather than US election officials.

I watch him shouting, and consider these men and their socially conservative values, me and my socially liberal ones, brought here together in an unlikely union of drinking from real glassware and ceramic.

I consider my compadres further; deprived their rightful drinking hours, furious at the hand of the state in their lives and against their freedoms. In this instance, I partly agree with them. The restrictions in Cataluña, with people wearing masks even on a beach, are as extreme as anywhere I have seen – a prioritisation of vigilance above the science of ventilation. I agree with some of the objection, if not with all of the fury and indignation I find here. I wonder if people can arrive furiously at the right answer even with the wrong working-out; if that can accidentally provide a social good, or only harm? Perhaps any brake on the absolute power of a state, in itself, always has an implicit hidden use, even where we don't naturally see it. Perhaps that use makes itself known only at a later date, when the impulse to resist a state becomes more obviously useful. As with the bicycle, and also the road, dissent is a part of a permanent connectedness of everything, where no energy, emotion or act can ever be destroyed, it just rolls around, sending out its next ripple-effect.

BASILICA

LIKE A NEW MAN, I walk on down the street; no more the wobbling, creaking pedal under my foot. Slower, but more dependable, I move across an empty road, a wet square. A small church calls to me; Basilica de la Mercè.

Inside the smell of old oak is up off the empty pews. The hymn books have all been taken away, replaced with QR codes and instructions for how to download them. Above me the words; Redemptrix, Gloriae. I look around at the icons, watching down so sad and holy, and the gleaming steel pipes of a church organ, silent but rising into the darkness. The yellow-red of the Catalan colours – apparently religious, not political, but they make their point – hang from a lectern.

A woman in a warm coat sits alone and silent at the front, beneath the altar. In my mind she joins with other images, the other portraits that I keep seeing and just can't shake, for in them seems to be some of the eternity of who we are about this globe: The father, singing a song hopefully at his crying child in a pram. The entwined fingers of an old couple, glanced quickly as once I rolled by in a small village, and on a bench, they held hands ridged with loose olive skin and turquoise veins. The kid with a bicycle, pulling a high wheelie down the centre of an empty street. I keep seeing all of it, imprinted like a statement on the meaning of this time. Again, that question; What comes next? What comes next for the way that I lived, what survives of the world and ways I grew up in?

Sometimes I think one day I might like to hit the switch, not in a church but more likely a mosque; to submit and pray to a system where it can all make sense at last; a belief to explain away all that I cannot believe. But I'm not there yet, I do not want the world to make sense until the world makes sense.

Quietly, I walk to the side aisle where rows of small candles gutter. I take out my wallet, my fifty cents change from the café. I drop it to the donation box. I light my candle from another already burning soft. I watch its wick spark and then flame. My mind moves, and I pay attention to the first things – thoughts I will read as wishes – that it settles on, making these, I suppose, my quiet prayer. My concluding thoughts, desires. This above all else; for me, for everyone.

Health, safe passage.

Fox, Finch & Tepper

Fox, Finch & Tepper is an independent publisher based in Bath. We began by resurrecting under-celebrated, beautifully written books with a strong sense of place. With 'Iberia' we embark on broadening our mission by publishing original works of fiction and narrative non-fiction as well as reissues. Whatever we publish, our publications are books we adore and believe in and that we feel deserve to be read and loved by many readers.

Books published by Fox, Finch & Tepper: